Hydrotherapy in Pediatrics

To accomplish great things, we must not only act but also dream,
not only plan but also believe.

Anon.

This book is dedicated to
'Mac'
who introduced me to the Halliwick Method which
opened up a whole new world, and a wealth of
opportunities and experiences.

Hydrotherapy in Pediatrics

Margaret Reid Campion
Lecturer in Physiotherapy
Western Australian Institute of Technology, Perth

AN ASPEN PUBLICATION®
Aspen Systems Corporation,
Rockville, Maryland
1986

Library of Congress Cataloging in Publication Data

Campion, Margaret Reid.
Hydrotherapy in pediatrics

"An Aspen publication."
References: p.243
Includes index.
1. Hydrotherapy in children. I. Title.
(DNLM: 1. Hydrotherapy - in infancy & childhood.
WB 520 C196h)
RJ53.H9C36 1985 615.8'53 85-1394
ISBN 0-87189-106-9

Aspen Systems Corporation, 1600 Research Boulevard, Rockville, Maryland 20850.

Library of Congress Catalog Card Number: 85-1394
ISBN: 0-87189-106-9

Printed in Great Britain

CONTENTS

FOREWORDS

Hydrotherapy is enjoying a resurgence of interest and enhanced popularity in English-speaking countries – a popularity it has always sustained in France and Germany. It is therefore timely that Margaret Reid Campion, well known in Great Britain and Australia not only as a highly esteemed paediatric physiotherapist and teacher but also as an ardent exponent of the Halliwick Method of swimming for the disabled, should prepare a monograph on this and related topics, suitable for all ages.

Coupled with the belated recognition that handicapped people – 'special people' – derive as much pleasure from water fun as the rest of us, there is accumulating evidence of the specific value of hydrotherapy in a variety of handicaps.

The author has unrivalled experience of all aspects of hydrotherapy and this book can be commended as an authoritatively practical account.

John Wilson PhD, FRCP
Consultant Neurologist
Hospital for Sick Children
Great Ormond Street
London

Margaret Reid Campion has been a leader in hydrotherapy and paediatrics (on two continents). Evidence of her contributions to both fields may be found in her publications and in the popularity of her lecture/workshops in Australia, Britain and elsewhere. Since 1962, she has been involved in the work of the Association of Swimming Therapy whose principal aim is to teach the disabled to swim through the technique known as the Halliwick Method. This method has gained widespread acceptance as an important therapeutic modality.

Currently there is a resurgence of interest in hydrotherapy in Australia, evidenced not only by a substantial increase in the number of therapeutic pools established both in hospitals and private practices, but also by increases in medical referrals for this activity.

This book has been written to assist those who now wish to expand their skills by the effective use of water and swimming as a therapeutic and recreational medium. The work is the result of twenty years of experience in hydrotherapy and paediatric physiotherapy, and is unique in its demonstration of the fun and enjoyment which can be an integral part of physical treatment. Most people like water, wish to learn to swim, and gain a considerable sense of achievement as they learn to understand and control the very different forces acting on their bodies. Physiotherapists often use play as a motivating force in the rehabilitation of children, and in this book Mrs Reid Campion clearly and concisely demonstrates ways in which play activities can be directed toward physical treatment in water.

Although *Hydrotherapy in Paediatrics* has been written with children in mind, there is much information that can be adapted to the rehabilitation of the adult in water, and there is no doubt that this book is a valuable addition to the literature on hydrotherapy which has been available to practitioners and students.

Dr L. Twomey
Principal, School of Physiotherapy
Western Australian Institute of Technology
National President, Australian
Physiotherapy Association

PREFACE AND ACKNOWLEDGEMENTS

In recent years interest in the development of water activity for able-bodied and disabled persons has markedly increased. My fortuitous meeting with Mr James McMillan MBE came at a moment in my life when my personal experience and ability in water and my expertise in hydrotherapy were running along parallel lines. Mr McMillan's work and ideas unified my approach to the medium of water as a means of rehabilitation. I have been increasingly involved in the teaching of therapeutic and recreational activity in water ever since.

This book has stemmed from many years of practical work in water with all types of disabilities of any age and severity, and it is hoped that it will prove valuable to those physiotherapists interested in water activity for the disabled.

A book of this nature is not the work of one person. I owe a great debt of gratitude to many people; most importantly to all those disabled persons who have, throughout the years, taught me so much, provided me with encouragement as they developed skills in the water and cheerfully submitted to my ministrations. To all those who attended my courses and contributed so much to my learning I say a deeply felt 'thank you'. In more personal terms I wish to thank all those friends and colleagues who encouraged me to write this book: Jenny Cook and Valda Wilson who assisted with the typing and corrections; my daughter Carol who patiently typed and retyped the final draft; and June Rankine-Wilson who spared no effort and willingly read and re-read my words and gave so much valuable criticism and advice. My husband Peter bore the brunt of long hours of loneliness as I laboured over the script, and gave much helpful criticism, provided endless cups of coffee and all the valuable information included in the Appendix on the anatomy of the skull, embryologic, neonatal and infant development of that part of the human body. Wendy Olford's skills as an illustrator are much appreciated. I am also deeply indebted to Danny Mahoney whose ideas on the teaching of swimming strokes have proved invaluable and so successful over the years.

Finally, I wish to thank the publishers. Their patience and encouragement throughout the task or writing this book were considerable, especially those of Mr Selwyn Taylor who supported me from the time he invited me to write the book until its publication.

Many of the ideas contained in this book may be adapted and used in the treatment of disabled adults. The basic principles and skills are as necessary for adults as they are for children. Music and rhythm play a part in rehabilitation and there is an infinite variety of compositions that may be used appropriately for older age groups.

INTRODUCTION

Water is fun! The majority of people enjoy water and it is an integral part of life.

The unborn child exists in a liquid environment and after birth appears to have no fear of water. Babies find pleasure in the warmth of their bath and in the feel of water. Later, as the ability to move actively develops, kicking and splashing make bathing a happy part of the daily routine. Playing with toys and other objects while in water is also a source of pleasure, activity and learning in the young child's life. Swimming, however, is a skill that has to be learnt. Prior to the 1970s the emphasis on instruction in water safety focused on school-age children. But now slowly — too slowly many would argue — there is a shift of emphasis towards the pre-school, toddler and infant age groups (Best, 1979). The reasons for this shift in emphasis are many and include protection against the risk of drowning together with the realisation that there are psychological and recreational benefits to be gained.

Unfortunately the situation has been exploited, and some unscrupulous persons with little knowledge of the physical, mental and emotional development of children have in recent years commercialised the teaching of swimming to the very young. A more responsible attitude is slowly emerging, and with it the recognition that if enjoyment of water and learning to swim are part and parcel of able-bodied children's lives, so they should also be part and parcel of the lives of disabled children. Water allows all of us to achieve marvellous feats of movement which can be performed on land only with difficulty, if at all. For the disabled child water may be the only environment in which total independence can be achieved.

Campion (1983, p.181) suggests that 'children who are handicapped need not be denied the delight of movement. Physical activity on land may be hard for such children, but in the water they came into their own.' All children need to experience active movement if they are to develop. The lack of such movement for disabled children may well be an important factor in retarding their development. Water as a medium for activity is a most useful means of widening the experience of such children.

The word hydrotherapy is derived from the Greek words *hydor* (water) and *therapeia* (healing) (Duffield, 1976, p.1). Hydrotherapy is as old as the history of mankind (Finnerty and Corbitt, 1973, p.1), and information on activity in water for both therapeutic and recreational purposes has been documented despite the fact that the popularity of this modality has fluctuated through the ages. One authority (Behrend, 1960) believes that the use of hydrotherapy antedates that of all other modalities employed in physical medicine. The past shows us that many forms of treatment once greeted with enthusiasm have long since been abandoned, while hydrotherapy has continued even though the rationale is largely empirical. But this picture is changing. New knowledge regarding the physiology of hydrotherapy and new techniques using patterns of movement adapted to water and more water-specific exercises are ensuring that hydrotherapy is becoming increasingly accepted as a medium for rehabilitation in its own right. That it should be considered thus is, in the author's opinion, correct. To go into water — one of only two environments available to the human — is a unique experience. Here the body is simultaneously acted upon by two forces — gravity (or downthrust) and buoyancy (or upthrust) — providing us with the possibility of three-dimensional exercise not available in the medium of air, and allowing movement and non-weight-bearing activities to occur before they are possible on land.

With greater understanding of the advantages of activity in water, increasing numbers of facilities are being provided, and therapists are becoming both interested and skilled in the application of techniques and more aware of the benefits of swimming as an adjunct to fitness and performance generally. It has been suggested (Scrutton and Gilbertson, 1975) that paediatric hydrotherapy has local and general aspects. While agreeing, the author believes that if hydrotherapy is considered to be purely remedial, it loses some value when taking children into water because children tend to find exercises as such boring. However, if the exercise can be hidden in an activity that is fun, the programme for the child becomes of interest and both therapeutic and recreational aspects have been incorporated.

With this in mind, the ensuing chapters have been written as a guide to achieving therapeutic aims. In addition, it is hoped they will prove useful to those teaching swimming to disabled children, so that, like their able-bodied peers, they can not only cope with the risks attendant on being in water, but also benefit from its physiological, psychological, social and recreational aspects.

A recent comment on the Halliwick Method emphasised the functional value of the many activities and games. This is indeed so, but the author trusts that the fun, laughter and pleasure are not lost in the effort to provide function.

Much of the author's knowledge and experience has been shaped and developed by the Halliwick Method. This method of teaching the disabled to swim was the brainchild of Mr James McMillan MBE, President Emeritus of the Association of

Swimming Therapy. It has become world renowned, and the contribution that 'Mac' has made, and is continuing to make, not only to swimming for the disabled but to hydrotherapy, is immense. I am deeply grateful to him for his help and guidance over many years.

Chapter 1

INTRODUCTION TO ACTIVITY IN WATER

THE VALUE OF ACTIVITY IN WATER

The value of activity in water for the able-bodied has been well documented and needs little mention in this book. For the disabled, however, such information is either confined to texts on hydrotherapy or is described by authors, swimming teachers and physical educationalists who are largely concerned with teaching the able-bodied child to swim. Teaching the disabled to swim has become part of the hydrotherapist's work only in comparatively recent times, and it should be stated that in general, normal teaching methods are not successful with the disabled. The nature of the handicap must be well understood and due allowance made for the problems it involves.

Elkington (1978) states that swimming is an essential part of every child's physical education and suggests that the value of swimming is for survival, fitness and fun. These reasons apply equally to the disabled child, for if we hope to integrate the disabled into as normal a life as possible, then they too must be able to survive, achieve maximum fitness and enjoy the element of water. The attitude to water of most disabled children is one of pleasure and enjoyment. The desire to learn to swim is invariably present and once the art is learned a sense of achievement is experienced. Consequently confidence and self-respect are enhanced, and since swimming and competing with the able-bodied become a reality, social benefits accrue.

The properties of buoyancy and turbulence offered by water enable the disabled child not only to move with greater freedom, but may also make it possible to execute movement which would be impossible on land. It is probable that the general slowing down encountered in water may give the child time to react and appreciate how to use the body (Scrutton and Gilbertson, 1975, p.138).

Studies of the relationship between movement and aspects of intellectual development have been carried out by many workers and indicate that limitations of active movement, from whatever cause, are likely to retard perceptual development, of which body image and spatial awareness are part. Rosenbloom (1975) takes the point first made by Held (1965) that neither passive movement nor no movement can be substituted for the active movement of the body and its parts in the normal development of perceptual and visuomotor skill.

Children with disorders of movement may also have impairment of body image and spatial awareness. The appreciation of three-dimensional space is often difficult for such children. Lack of experience of active movement in the normal environment in many instances accounts for these difficulties.

In water, movement is made easier and experience of that movement may help to improve the child's awareness and understanding. Aids and appliances necessary on land can be discarded in this medium and this can result in changes in the attitude of many children, leading to joy and pleasure in the newly discovered freedom of movement. This discovery of the body as a whole unit plays a significant part in the child's overall development.

Once the child can swim, the opportunities for socialisation are enhanced both in the family situation and amongst the child's peers, and other aquatic sports can be undertaken and enjoyed as the major skill of swimming is achieved. Thus, to the great advantage of the child, horizons widen.

INTRODUCING CHILDREN TO WATER

For all human beings — creatures of land — water is a strange element. Therefore it is important to familiarise the infant with water at an early stage. This can be done at bathtime and continued through early childhood. The need to be mentally adjusted to the element of water is essential for any activity that takes place in it. Development of the child from an early apedal existence to bipedal locomotion has taken place against gravity, so when entering water movement patterns used on land become difficult. In addition to the gross postural confusion that may result, tension, anxiety and fear may be present. The loss of datum points as known on land and the seeming restriction of breathing only add to the anxiety. It follows, therefore, that activities should be presented in such a manner that adjustment to the new environment is facilitated.

Adjustment to water — physical and mental

Balance problems arise because the human body is not in perfect symmetry. For the able-bodied this asymmetry is small, and balance and stability are more readily acquired. But for the disabled asymmetry is much more severe, and balance becomes a serious problem. In addition to a natural anxiety and fear, the disabled will have a number of other problems with which to contend. Due to the disability, asymmetry in shape and/or density may be markedly altered. There may also be an acute fear of falling, difficulties with respiration, communication and comprehension, an inability to create movement as required, or an inability to control involuntary movement.

Thus it can be seen that adjustment to the element of water is of prime importance. Such adjustment comes through a knowledge of the properties and characteristics of water, the ability to adjust to its feel, its turbulence, its buoyancy and its weight, as these all affect the body balance. This knowledge can be taught through games and activities that are fun and combine therapeutic goals and recreational skills.

This mental adjustment is as important for the therapist as it is for the children taken into the water. There is no doubt that such adjustment by the therapist plays a large part in reassuring the child. Verbal assurances such as 'It's all right, I am holding you' are not usually acceptable to the child. Children are only too aware of any instability or lack of control on the part of the person handling them. Therefore mental adjustment should continue throughout a large part of programmes of activity in water, though as the child acquires confidence and an increasing number of skills, the need for it decreases.

Every game or activity is developed to include the teaching of these skills and consequently facilitating mental adjustment. The ways in which this is done can include gaining control of breathing, balance, head position and movement. The ability to relax and gain a feel for the water and movement within it, by becoming aware of one's body image and the relationships of the body parts to each other and in space, can be developed. The nature of the total teaching environment, including the facilities and equipment, must be considered.

Breathing control

Good breathing control is essential for all activity in water including swimming. It is frightening to inhale water and this can be prevented by encouraging breathing out, or 'blowing'. Such action should form the background for all activities. If water comes near the face or the face near water, instruct the child to 'blow'. Breathing control needs to become regular and rhythmical not only when the face is above the surface, but particularly when it is submerged. To assist control in the latter circumstance, the child should be encouraged either to exhale through the nostrils or mouth or to hum. Simply requiring the child to hold the breath can cause tension within the body, and this tension will cause an alteration in the body shape and thus in the balance of the body in water.

Encouragement of breathing control must continue at all times and 'blow' should be the word most frequently heard in the pool. Such an essential skill is not readily achieved by some disabled children, and frequently advanced skills may have been acquired while breathing control as an automatic and effective action is still lacking.

Blowing is also a prerequisite for head control since the blowing action helps bring the head forward and assists in creating forward rotation around the centre of buoyancy. The strong expiration of air from the lungs as the face goes forwards ensures that the following inspiration will be greater. The chest will be working against the pressure of water, aiding expiration, resisting inspiration, though the degree to which this occurs depends on the position of the body in the water.

Some children may have a lowered vital capacity and can at first experience some distress from the pressure of the water on their chests. In these cases positions should be used where the chest is not fully immersed, for example lying supine where the anterior part of the chest wall can be clear of the surface. A few relaxed deep breaths will assist in gaining some immediate relief of any anxiety, and as breathing control is gained the child will not mind the body position being changed so that the chest is totally submerged.

Relaxation

Relaxation is as essential for activity in water as it is in any other aspect of life. Stress, fear, anxiety, pain and muscle spasm, create tension (Mitchell, 1977). For the disabled person, the easing of tension (whatever its cause) will be of considerable advantage in relation to exercise in water. Swimming with greater freedom of movement and activity becomes possible once relaxation has been obtained.

Relaxation is achieved by the following means.

1. The support given to the body by the buoyancy of the water offsets much of the effect of gravity and promotes relaxation and reduces pain if present (Duffield, 1976).
2. The weightlessness experienced by the body when it is placed in water also induces relaxation (Harris and McInnes, 1963).
3. The warmth of the water will help to bring about overall relaxation and the relief of tension particularly where aches and pains are present (Harris and McInnes, 1963; Duffield, 1976).

The initial introduction to water may produce anxiety, fear and stress. For the disabled there will be additional problems of a physical nature. A description of, and methods of dealing with anxiety, fear and stress are given elsewhere in the text (see pp. 32 and 43). Of prime importance are:

(a) mental adjustment to the element of water,
(b) good handling,
(c) the provision of appropriate and enjoyable activities,
(d) establishing a rapport,
(e) creating an appropriate atmosphere.

In order to achieve these aims, the therapist must understand the properties and characteristics of water and be able to cope with these personally (see p. 14). A knowledge of anatomy, physiology, pathology, child development and of hydrotherapeutic exercise will play a vital role in promoting relaxation in the disabled children taken into water.

Relaxation then shares an equal role with breathing control and balance as essential elements for activity in water. When any of these is lacking, or has been only partially acquired, the others are difficult to achieve since clear influences are all so closely interwoven.

A knowledge of the effects of altered shape and density on the body when it is placed in water enables the therapist to predict what the balance and rotational problems of any child taken into water will be. Where possible, this knowledge should be used to impart to the child ways in which balance can be acquired even before entering the water. Thus armed, the child may well be less anxious and thereby less tense. Mental adjustment has begun, and with it a more relaxed approach.

Slow, rhythmic swinging and rolling movements promote relaxation; rotation around the longitudinal body axis reduces spasticity (Sullivan *et al.*, 1982). Similarly, bilateral movements performed slowly and rhythmically in supported supine lying may be useful (Harris and McInnes, 1963). The support may be provided by floats or, more appropriately, particularly with young children, by the therapist using the backing hold (see p. 55). Gentle swaying of the child by the therapist as in 'Seaweed' (see p. 136) further encourages relaxation, and the activities 'Bells' (see p. 98) and 'Rag Dolls' (see p. 104) are other examples of swinging movements. When using either lateral rotation or rolling, the movements should be performed slowly and rhythmically with smooth handling by the therapist. In teaching such rotation, the author has found it invaluable to break the task down into its components and encourage the rolling action with the body in both flexion and extension. The use of music can prove valuable. Even if it is only the therapist who hums an appropriate rhythm, relaxation and smoother movement in both the child and therapist may result. But in all cases where tension is likely to be a problem the therapist is advised to spend some part of the initial sessions in working towards its alleviation.

Head control

The importance of the development of head control in the young child has been a subject of research by many workers who indicate that it forms the basis for development of all functions. Failure to develop adequate head control leads to the inability to position the head in space and to work against gravity. As a result, eye–hand co-ordination, visual acuity and balance are affected, as well as other gross and fine motor skills (Rosenbloom, 1975). 'Where the head goes the body follows': if this is true on land, then it is equally true in water where the head controls the position of the body and feet entirely. Thus the need for good head control is essential.

In the vertical plane the head must be kept slightly forward to maintain the upright position. Any movement that takes the head too far forward or backward will cause a loss of balance with an upswing of the legs opposite to the movement of the head. A forward movement of the head will cause the legs to swing up behind the swimmer, who will become prone in the water, and a backward movement will cause the feet to swing up so that the swimmer is in the supine lying position.

Since it is harder to create vertical rotation around the centre of buoyancy, good head control is critical. In the 'ball' shape (see Fig. 4, p. 21), the body will swing more rapidly when any movement of the head takes place. In fact, if a swimmer is in the vertical and then collapses the body down into a 'ball' by bending the knees to the chest and placing the hands around the knees, water will rotate the body forward until it is floating face down with just the thoracic spine above the surface. To counter this rotational effect, strong extension of the head is required. Vertical rotation requires strong flexion of the trunk, hips, knees and cervical spine, with flexion of the shoulders in abduction followed by precise balance of the head over the body to maintain the upright position.

It is also possible to create a roll in a lateral direction by using the head, but if such a roll occurs due to other disturbing forces, then the head can be used to counter this rotation. For instance, if the body in supine is rolled to one side manually, or because of other disturbing forces, the swimmer can use the head to bring the body back to a flat position.

Balance control

Balance control is acquired through learning to cope with the body shape and the rotational patterns that occur as a consequence of altered shape, and by adjustments to the effects of buoyancy. It is necessary to appreciate turbulent effects and to attain maintenance of balance and stability against this disturbing force. Activities introduce the child to turbulence and teach this control first in stable shapes, then, as control develops, in less stable shapes.

Feel of water

'Feel of water' includes not only the sensation of water on the skin and its all-encompassing nature, but the drag effect produced by turbulence which is appreciated most at the distal part of the limbs. Having the 'feel' of water is also demonstrated by being able to work with the therapist without gripping for support and later by the ability to submerge confidently, breathing out in a controlled manner.

Discovering that water has weight, that it can be leant against and used as a force against which work can take place, assists in understanding its characteristics — thus improving confidence.

Movement

Movement in water as well as balance and stability are important. To change from the positions of standing, sitting, kneeling and lying in water and to walk forwards, backwards and sideways, to jump, turn and roll are prerequisites for independence in the medium.

Body image and spatial relationships

The development of body image and spatial relationships can be encouraged or improved in water. The child can learn body dimensions, and become more aware of the limbs and where they are in space and in relation to the rest of the body. The extremes of posture in water — the 'ball' and 'stick' — and the need to change from one extreme to the other to create forward rotation improve awareness of body image.

ENVIRONMENT

The importance of the environment in which the child will participate in water activity will undoubtedly have a bearing on progress. A specially designed facility would seem ideal. However, when thinking in terms of hydrotherapy, those concerned with design and construction usually produce complicated plans and equipment. The less elaborate the design, the more useful it becomes for both therapy and recreation, and any equipment required should be both simple and easily removed from the pool.

There is, then, little or no need for elaborate pool design or equipment when taking disabled children into water. Although an increasing number of pools are being built, many older facilities may be used satisfactorily by those wishing to give disabled children experience of water activity.

The following points to be considered about the environment are not intended to be a manual of pool design, but outline factors that have been found to be important when taking children into water.

1. Water and air temperatures.
2. Water depth.
3. Size of pool, expanse of surface of water, height of bathside above the water.
4. Noise factors.
5. Hoists, changing rooms and showers.
6. Lighting.
7. Surfaces.
8. Turbulence.

Water and air temperatures

When taking disabled children into water, the temperature of the water and air should be between 30°C and 34°C (86°F and 93°F). This is warmer than the 27°C (80°F) advocated by Elkington (1978) and not as warm as the average temperature of hydrotherapy pools, which is 35.5°–36.6°C (96°–98°F).

If the water is too warm, it proves exhausting and uncomfortable. However, if it is too cold, inhibition of movement may occur, and since movement can also be diminished by the child's disability, heat loss to the water becomes a problem.

Skin temperature is normally 33.5°C (92°–93°F) and water temperature above this will feel warm to hot, and below it cool to cold.

Air temperature should be slightly lower than that of the water to allow gentle cooling. The rate of cooling of a body in a given time is proportional to the difference in temperature between the body and its surroundings. The greater the difference in temperature, the greater will be the rate of cooling — this is Newton's Law of cooling.

Humidity is another factor to be considered. If the humidity and atmospheric temperature are high, the body cannot lose heat by conduction, convection and radiation. If the body has difficulty in losing heat, it can be most uncomfortable for both children and staff. Proper control of temperature thus becomes vital.

Water depth

Vertical balance in water becomes a critical factor at two-thirds of a person's height, or when the water level reaches approximately to the lower end of the sternum. For an optimum working depth, a further 6 inches (15.24 cm) of water, bringing the level to shoulder height, is adequate. It is suggested that a depth that varies between 0.84 m and 1.42 m is ideal — the shallower range being advisable if children are to work in the pool (Skinner and Thomson, 1983, p.28).

The advantages of deeper water usually outweigh those of the shallower depth. If a base is required, the therapist can provide this with the thighs. The most stable position for the therapist to work in is that of a square, and thus a ready-made human platform is available to the child.

A sloping floor with a gradient of 1:20 or 1:15 provides useful water depths in which a variety of activities can be undertaken. Some authorities suggest a stepped floor to the pool, but experience shows that this can be disconcerting to the patient and therapist alike. However clearly their edges are delineated, the steps may not be seen readily and a feeling of insecurity is engendered. The author believes that the advantages are heavily outweighed by the disadvantages and that a gently sloping floor is ideal.

Size of pool

The dimensions of a pool are frequently governed

by cost, and it is not often that the ideal criteria of pools suitable to the child's age and ability are met. This should not prevent children being taken into water, especially on the one-to-one basis required with the disabled child, at least until they are competent in water.

However, an expanse of water will seem frightening to a child. Even quite small pools may have this effect. This anxiety can be overcome by the therapist ensuring that the surface is broken by floating objects, by being in the water ready to assist the child's entry, and by facing into a corner or working across the shortest distance of the pool. This last strategy provides short-distance focal points.

The height of the bathside from the water line, if more than a few inches, can prove worrying to the child. Once again with the therapist in the water prior to the child's entry, this particular problem can be avoided. Too great a distance decreases the ease with which the child may enter and exit over the side of the pool, and increases the difficulties of handling in an emergency.

Noise factor

Pools tend to be noisy places where much activity, laughter, shouting and splashing occurs. This too may produce anxiety and tension in both able-bodied and disabled children. The latter may have retained the Moro reflex or have an exaggerated startle reflex where head control and postural stability are limited or absent, so can find a noisy pool particularly disturbing. In these cases, children can be helped to tolerate and finally cope with this through a one-to-one relationship with the therapist leading to progressive mental adjustment and balance restoration.

Hoists, changing rooms and showers

In the author's experience, poolside lifts are expensive and of limited value. They may be useful if older, extremely disabled children are to be taken into the pool. If a lift is to be provided, the hydraulic hoist run on water pressure is probably the best, having a smooth lifting and lowering action. Overhead gantry-type hoists tend to swing about and such action may be disturbing to the children. On the whole, when working with children it is possible to get them into and out of the pool manually if necessary. However, an independent means of entry and exit should be the aim, and various methods are described later in the text (see pp. 43 and 47).

Changing rooms should be warm and have space for wheelchairs and shower chairs to manoeuvre. Changing tables should be provided since many of the disabled will require help with undressing and dressing, and a suitable system to avoid mixing of clothing and apparatus should be devised.

Lighting

It is essential that at all times the entire water area to its full depth is visible so that activities being undertaken can be clearly seen and modifications made to incorrect movement patterns. Since the children will also be required to submerge, and may well swim underwater, it is vital in the interests of safety that they can be clearly seen. Thus, lighting in the pool must be designed in such a way as to avoid as much as possible refraction and reflection which mar vision underwater.

Non-slip surfaces

Non-slip surfaces need to be provided on the floor of the pool, on the surrounding areas and in the changing rooms. There is always a danger of slipping on the wet bathside surface, and where balance is precarious and crutches and walking sticks with rubber tips may be used, the provision of a non-slip surface is vital. A feeling of security is engendered by this type of floor. For the floor of the pool, small mosaic-type tiles which have a matt finish usually provide the best surface. Tiled surfaces are easier to maintain and this is important where the presence of bacteria must be controlled.

Prevention of a build-up of turbulence

For many disabled people, balance is difficult and the sensitivity to balance disturbance is acute. In water, where stability is not easily obtained, any factors which may add to the difficulties of gaining stability and balance should be avoided. Turbulence is one of these factors and is greatly increased in the pool where there are curves or rounded surfaces, steps and ramps and strong jets, both surface and underwater. It is advisable to have the side of the pool and the floor meet at a right-angle, to recess steps and ramps, and to reduce the flow through jets to a minimum.

A further point to consider in the provision of the right-angle where the side of the pool and the floor meet is that it allows ease of handling over the side of the pool for the therapist from a correct mechanical position.

Generally speaking, the pool environment should be simply designed and functional for both therapy and recreation. It should be bright and colourful and provide the appropriate temperatures and atmosphere to encourage the children in water activity.

BASIC PHYSICS AND ITS APPLICATION

If the principles of activity in water are to be

understood, a knowledge of the properties and characteristics of water is necessary. The physical properties are described in detail in the literature, usually under the headings of mass, weight, density, specific gravity, buoyancy, hydrostatic pressure, surface tension, refraction and viscosity (MacDonald, 1973; Skinner and Thomson, 1983).

The majority of readers will be familiar with such facts, and further description is inappropriate except where it has relevance to the subject matter of this book, where special points require emphasis, or where no mention of certain facts is made in the literature.

A number of the laws of hydrodynamics are deemed to be of major importance for an understanding of water and activity in the medium. Therefore the most essential of these are given in Table 1. From these hydrodynamic principles, a number of facts need to be grasped, and such understanding is a prerequisite for therapists preparing to take children into water.

Table 1 Laws of hydrodynamics (adapted from unpublished lecture material, J. McMillan, 1975)

Author	*Principle*
Archimedes (c.BC 287–212)	Relative density
Bougier (1746)	Metacentre
Bernoulli (1700–82)	Turbulence
Reynolds (1849–1912)	Flow
Prandtl (1875–1953)	Boundary layer
Froude (1810–79) and Zahm (1862–1945)	Friction
Pascal (1623–62)	Pressure

Archimedes Principle

This principle states that when a body is immersed in a fluid it experiences a buoyant force equal to the weight of the fluid which the body has displaced. The relative density of water is one. Thus any body of a density less than one will float.

The relative density of the human body varies with age. The infant or young child has a relative density of approximately 0.86 and so flotation is assured. The smaller the relative density, the easier it is to float. In adolescence and early adulthood the relative density of the body is approximately 0.97. The body can float, though to do so becomes more difficult. In the later years of life, with an increase in adipose tissue (Smith and Bierman, 1973), the relative density of the body tends to return towards 0.86 and so it becomes easier to float again.

Each individual part and tissue of the body has its own relative density. Some body parts, such as the arms, are less dense and float easily, while other parts, such as the legs, are more dense and tend to sink. The importance of studying the density of the person undertaking activity in water becomes apparent. In certain disabilities there are marked alterations in the density of body parts, as for example changes in density in the lower limbs of children with spina bifida or muscular dystrophy.

Bougier's Theorem

A body immersed in water is subjected to two opposing forces — gravity and buoyancy. If these forces are equal, then the body will float, and if these forces are directionally opposite to each other, no rotation will occur. However, if the forces of gravity and buoyancy are unequal and unaligned, then rotation occurs and continues until such time as the two forces are once more in alignment.

When these forces are applied to the human body it can be seen that, when floating, the body is balanced and in equilibrium. However, if a part of the body is taken above the surface of the water, the balance of the body is upset as the forces of gravity and buoyancy are no longer equal and directionally opposite. The body will rotate until the two forces are aligned once more.

Due to disability, some people may have a body part that remains above the surface and as a result the body will rotate. The child with a marked pattern of flexion with abduction of the shoulder of an affected arm may have difficulty in keeping the limb below the surface of the water and must learn to counteract the rotational movement in addition to acquiring an improved arm pattern.

Bernoulli's Theorem

This theorem is concerned with the relation between fluid pressure and fluid velocity along a streamline in the steady flow of a frictionless fluid which has a constant density. Part of the theorem is an expression of energy. The total energy of a particle of water at any moment is the sum of its energies, which are:

(a) pressure energy,
(b) potential energy,
(c) kinetic energy.

The term turbulence denotes the existence of eddies, and these follow in the wake of an object moving through a fluid. If the movement is slow, then the flow of the particles is nearly parallel to the object and proceeds in smooth continuous curves. With an increase in speed, eddies occur and the energy contained in these eddies is dissipated, reducing the pressure and increasing the drag on the body. This low-pressure area has a suction effect and it is into such an area a body can fall. The shape of the body greatly influences the production of turbulence.

Turbulence, then, may be used both to assist and resist movement in pool therapy. Since any movement creates turbulence and a drag effect, the therapist must be careful about the manner and speed of movement around the person being treated in order not to cause a loss of balance. The drag effect will also have a damping effect on involuntary movement.

Reynolds' Theorem

Reynolds' work on flow indicates that there are two types of flow:

(a) laminar flow,
(b) turbulent flow.

In the former the flow is of streamlines of molecules in even and regular patterns. In the latter case the movement of the molecules is rapid, random and not streamlined; this type of flow creates return movements and eddies. Activity in water can be made more difficult by changing from a streamlined movement to unstreamlined movement (Duffield, 1976). For some disabled persons the inability to change the body shape may mean that work is taking place in the more difficult unstreamlined situation. The work of Reynolds helps with appreciating the theory of boundary layer which follows.

Prandtl's Theorem

When a fluid is flowing past a body or surface, a layer of fluid can be seen adjacent to the surface and the velocity of this fluid in relation to the surface is reduced so as to be non-existent. This region is called boundary layer. Much of the theory of boundary layer is based on the work of Prandtl and others who undertook flow research in the earlier part of this century. The importance of this from the therapist's point of view is mainly in that techniques for exit from a pool or river incorporating this theory can be taught, thus ensuring the person's complete safety. For instance, the fastest flow in a river will be at its centre. As the water gets close to the banks, the rate of flow is slowed until close to or against the bank there is an area of little or no flow. In exiting from the river, the child must learn to keep in this area and to lift the legs high and clear of the water as the forward movement over the side is carried out, otherwise the child may find the body being dragged back into the water. To a lesser extent, the same situation arises in the pool. Turbulence created by the movement of the water equates with that of the river, and there is an area of little or no flow against the side of the pool. The technique of getting out of the water can be taught in the pool situation thus ensuring the safety of the swimmer (see also p. 46).

Froude–Zahm's experiments

The work of these two scientists was directed towards the measurement of skin friction of a body passed through water and through air. The results of their work showed that under similar conditions skin friction was proportional to the densities of the two fluids. Skin friction was found to be 790 times greater in water than in air. The amount of energy required to perform movement in water is in a ratio of 790:1. This impedance to movement in water has an important part to play. It provides a situation where more active exercise can be undertaken. Along with turbulent effect, it damps down involuntary movements and, if balance is lost, the falling movement is retarded and time allowed for the person to exert voluntary control to regain the original position.

Pascal's Law

Pascal's Law states that fluid pressure is exerted equally at any level in a horizontal direction; that is, pressure is equal at a constant depth. However, pressure increases with depth and with the density of the fluid.

Development of the human being against gravity

The development of the human individual occurs against the constant force of gravity. Strong but unseen, gravity affects all movements from birth on. On land, the human being uses data points of resistance against which the body is able to thrust. When placed in water, such data points are removed and balance must be related to a new data point — the centre of buoyancy of the body.

Important considerations for activity in water

The following facts must be considered and understood if exercise in water is to be successful.

1. Shape and density are critical factors in responding to immersion in water.
2. There are two planes of rotation in water.
3. There are two extremes of posture of the human being in water.

Shape and density

Normal

Water reacts to the shape and density of any object placed in it, and floats the object according to these factors. This also applies to the human being when in water, and the variations in shape and density of different parts of the body account for the many and varied balance positions.

All human beings are asymmetrical to a greater or lesser degree and will have a balance problem in water. The majority float since the sum of the relative densities of the bones, tissues, teeth, organs and so on usually add up to a density less than the weight of water. Since body changes occur throughout life, there are times when it is easier to float than others. Babies and young children and the middle and older age groups float easily; the teenager and younger adult, especially the tall and lean, find it hard to float.

The person who has a disability will have marked alterations in shape and/or density. The importance of looking at shape and density and understanding the effects they will have on that body when in water cannot be too strongly stressed. It is vital that the therapist taking a child into water has considered these factors from all sides, including along the child's longitudinal axis.

From such observations and with knowledge of what happens to such altered shapes and density, programmes of activity can be developed to provide the child with every opportunity to achieve mental adjustment to the element of water and to acquire balance restoration.

If the child can comprehend explanations of the effect of altered shape and density, then it will be possible to commence mental adjustment prior to entering water.

Certain shapes are less stable than others in water (Table 2) and in practice it is found that the long thin shape is less stable, whereas a curled-up shape is more stable. The long thin shape (or 'stick') is unstable both in the vertical and horizontal. In the former it can be disturbed easily in all directions, and in the latter readily rotated around the longitudinal axis (Fig. 1a and b).

If the feet are placed wide apart sideways in the vertical position, some stability is provided laterally, but anteriorly and posteriorly the body is still easily displaced (Fig. 2).

If the body assumes a cube shape — a sitting posture with the legs apart and right-angles at hips, knees and ankles with the arms forwards — then increased stability is acquired and the head and arms can be used to assist the maintenance of this position against any disturbing influences. Thus

Table 2 Stable and unstable shapes in water (adapted from unpublished lecture material, J. McMillan, 1975)

Stable shapes
Cube
'Ball'

Unstable shapes
'Stick'
  vertical
  horizontal
Triangle — antero-posteriorly, some stability laterally

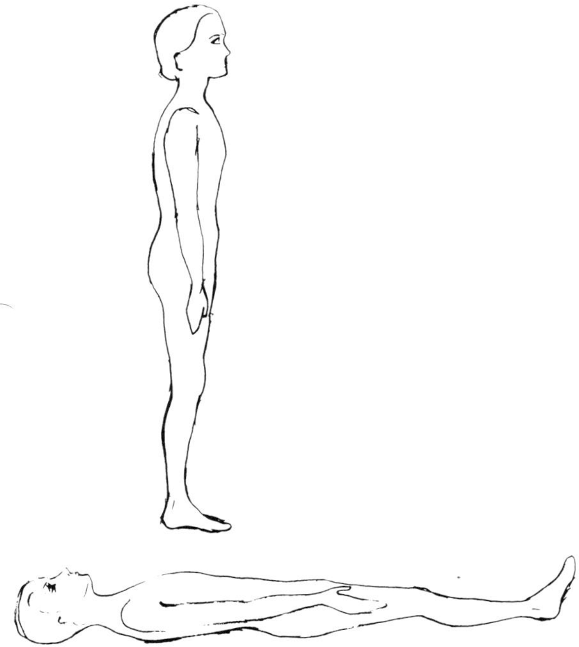

Fig. 1a and b *The 'stick' — vertical and horizontal.*

the body has become more stable in balance (Fig. 3).

When the body is collapsed further into a 'ball' shape with the hips and knees flexed against it and the hands held around the knees, it is immediately adjusted by the water, and floats curled up over the centre of buoyancy (Fig. 4). This shape, though it

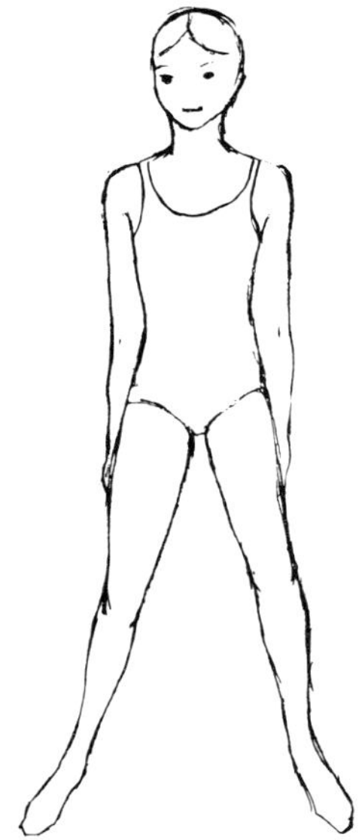

Fig. 2 *Triangular shape.*

may be easily disturbed, is the most stable in water, always returning to flotation over the centre of buoyancy with the thoracic spine showing above the surface. The precise floating position is always dependent on the individual's density, and some variations are seen in the size of the area of the back showing above the water.

Alterations in shape and density in the disabled (Table 3)
Those children whose disability does not affect their anatomical structure, for instance the blind

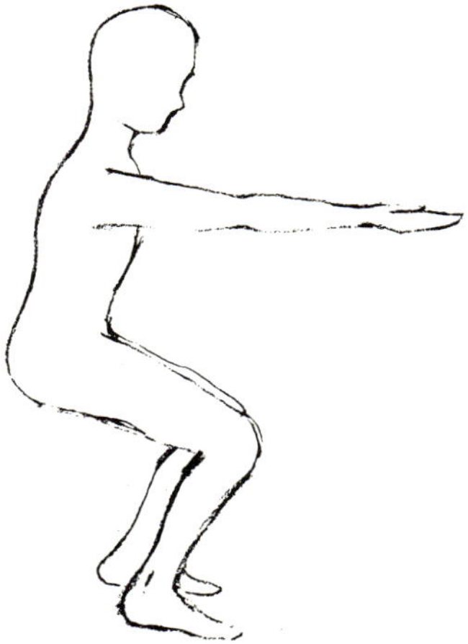

Fig. 3 *The 'cube'.*

Fig. 4 *The 'ball' shape.*

Table 3 Common alterations in body shape due to disability (adapted from unpublished lecture material, J. McMillan, 1975)

1. Unequal quadrilateral
2. Triangular
3. 'Sitting' or wheelchair
4. Adducted or 'scissor'
5. Extended
6. Higher centres of buoyancy and gravity
7. Neutral equilibrium

and the deaf, will, in common with the able-bodied population, present minimal alterations in shape and/or density. Their disability will need particular attention for reasons related to their individual sense problems. The majority of other disabilities will have (to varying degrees) alterations in shape and density, and the most common shapes seen are those following.

1. Unequal quadrilateral.
2. Triangular shape.
3. Sitting or wheelchair shape.
4. Adducted or scissor shape.
5. Extended shape.
6. Higher centres of buoyancy and gravity and, more rarely, the child who is in a state of neutral equilibrium.

Complications following from these shapes include markedly altered density, such as is found in spina bifida, and further asymmetry of shape due to being affected more in one part or side of the body, as in children with spastic quadriplegia or diplegia. The child with congenital deformities or absence of limbs and the amputee will have alterations in both shape and density.

Since it is easier to bring about alterations in shape in water, and because it is important for the balance and stability of the swimmer, activities which will encourage a more equal shape or teach control of the altered shape and density should be introduced immediately. Thus, it can be seen how necessary it is for the effects of shape and density to be understood.

1. *The unequal quadrilateral* (Fig. 5a). This is most commonly seen in the hemiplegic child, and activities that will increase extension on the affected side and introduce symmetry have been described in Chapter 2. The appropriate activities for other conditions where a similar situation arises are described with the individual condition.

The child with hemiplegia will tend to be shorter on the affected side and, when placed in water, will roll to that side due to a greater quality of upthrust beneath the unaffected side (Fig. 5b). The degree to which the body rolls is dependent on the degree of shortening on the affected side.

A similar rolling action may occur in quadriplegics where one side is considerably more affected than the other, or in children whose loss of density

Fig. 5a *An unequal quadrilateral.*

Fig. 5b *An unequal quadrilateral in a horizontal position rolling to the altered side.*

(particularly in the lower limbs) may be much more marked in one leg than the other.

2. *The triangular shape* (Fig. 6). The triangular shape is frequently seen in children with spastic diplegia where there is flexion at hips and knees and

Fig. 6a *Triangular shape.*

plantar flexion at the ankle (Fig. 6a). Some spastic quadriplegics who have insufficient hip flexion and who half-lie on a chair acquiring a high dorsal kyphosis can also be considered triangular in shape (Fig. 6b). Other rarer conditions may bring about a

Fig. 6b *Triangular shape.*

marked increase in hip flexion resulting in a similar triangular shape.

In water a triangle will float with its point downwards, and so it can be seen that these children should work in the vertical or supine lying position in the early stages of activity in water. To put the triangular-shaped person face downwards in water means that they not only have to cope with water which is trying to turn them over, but they may well have insufficient extension in the cervical and thoracic spine to get the face clear of the water. Rotational control is also important since such children are likely to be more affected on one side than the other.

3. *The sitting or wheelchair shape* (Fig. 7). The disabled child who has had to spend a considerable amount of time in a wheelchair may have contractures of hips and knees. In cases where spasticity is part of the condition, there may also be flexion contractures of the upper limbs. By virtue of the

Fig. 7 *The wheelchair shape.*

flexion contractures of the lower limbs, there is a more stable posture for activity in water, but such activity will be limited. For the child's own well-being and greater independence in water, active extension must be encouraged. Again, the child will probably have an asymmetrical distribution of contractures and once again rotational effects will need attention, together with the teaching of control.

4. *The adducted or scissor shape* (Fig. 8). Where the child has marked adduction or even 'scissored' legs, the rotation around the longitudinal axis is most obvious; therefore teaching control of lateral rotation should be commenced immediately, and activities which will alter shape through abduction of the legs need to be encouraged.

Fig. 8 *The adducted or 'scissor' shape.*

5. *The extended shape* (Fig. 9). Many disabled children present with a marked extensor pattern and can be described, when supine, as taking the shape of an inverted saucer. Such a shape, when supine in water, will be extended over the centre of buoyancy. Density may be different at one end of the body from the other, and the body will tend to sink at the heavier end. Again, if the distribution of the disabling condition is asymmetrical, rotation about the longitudinal axis will be present.

6. *Higher centres of buoyancy and gravity*. Certain disabling conditions mean that the child's centres of gravity and buoyancy are higher than is normal. Such children may be hydrocephalic or have a condition such as spina bifida or cerebral palsy where the upper trunk and arms are more developed than the lower trunk and legs. In these children it is important that control of vertical rotation is emphasised so that any movement of the head anteriorly or posteriorly, however slight, is

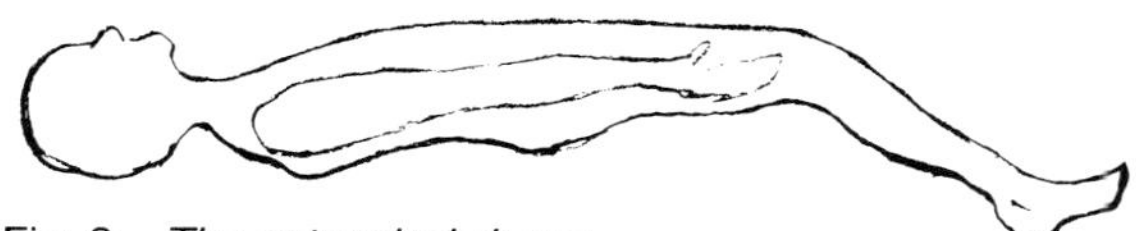

Fig. 9 *The extended shape.*

controlled, and no untoward loss of balance from the vertical occurs.

Neutral equilibrium

Some disabled children, by virtue of their shape and density, may float in a state of neutral equilibrium. They float easily in both supine and prone, but the latter position may impede respiration. Such children have rather large bodies with shorter arms and legs than normal, and lateral rotation around the longitudinal axis is difficult for them since the short levers give little assistance to rotation of the increased body size back to a safe breathing position. Density (as with shape) varies with each individual, but the person who is disabled is likely to have marked changes in this factor. Areas that are less dense will float more easily, whereas those that are more dense will have a tendency to sink.

Density equals weight divided by volume, and a significant reduction in weight rather than in volume has a greater effect on density.

Where limbs are atrophied due to disease, they are less dense and float easily. Children with spina bifida, paraplegia, anterior poliomyelitis, Guillian–Barre syndrome and similar conditions will find that their limbs will rise to the surface. Since in most instances the lower limbs are more affected than the upper limbs, the upswing of these limbs can be disturbing, emphasising the need for early control.

It has been shown that the head controls the feet and therefore teaching vertical rotational control is essential. Additionally, when supine in water, these children should extend the head in order to depress the lower limbs, thus the body is arched over its centre of buoyancy and can work more effectively.

Children who have congenital absence or deformities of limbs or who are amputees have both altered shape and density to a degree dependent on their disability, and control of the rotational effects must be effectively taught by use of the head and limbs.

The shape of the body can also be subjected to changes that are less obvious. Actions such as gripping, holding the breath and shutting the eyes tightly create tension which in turn alters the shape. These actions are frequently brought about by fear and anxiety, and the resulting tension is transferred to the body as a whole. In conditions such as athetosis where control of involuntary movements is not possible, changes of shape occur frequently.

It should now be evident how critical shape and density are when taking a disabled child into water. The therapist must not only study the child's shape and density, but be able (through knowledge of the properties of water) to predict what will happen to that shape and therefore plan a suitable programme which will provide the child with the most advantageous activities. These activities will be designed to teach control of rotational effects, and develop mental adjustment to water within a therapeutic and recreational programme.

Planes of rotation

Two planes of rotation occur in water — vertical and lateral — and can be compared to the vertical and lateral planes that occur on land and are closely associated with the development of the young child. Both can be observed in the development of the young child. When the head is turned the body follows and, later, the child lifts the head in supine and is gradually able to come to sitting. In the young child on land, lateral rotation occurs prior to vertical rotation and sitting up. In water vertical rotation is harder to achieve than lateral rotation.

If the child is to achieve total safety in water, the importance of teaching control in the two rotational planes cannot be sufficiently stressed. Rotational effects may occur due to movement of the head, arms and legs in addition to the changes the child's disability has wrought in the shape and density of the body.

The importance of head control and its part in creating or controlling vertical and lateral rotation are reiterated, and it must be emphasised again that breathing control is a prerequisite for head control and needs to be the background of all activities. Thus, 'blow' should be the commonest word heard in the pool area.

Vertical rotation

Vertical rotation occurs in a forward and backward direction around the body's centre of buoyancy and incorporates the ability to recover to the upright position from either supine or prone lying. The skill is required for total independence in water, and demonstrates the child's ability to recover to a safe breathing position.

The head has a vital role to play in vertical rotation. To achieve supine lying, the head is taken slowly backwards and as the action takes place the feet move forward and upward to the surface. Recovery from this position requires strong flexion of the cervical spine, trunk, hips and knees, with flexion of the shoulders in abduction followed by precise balance of the head over the body to maintain the upright position. If requiring prone lying, the head is moved slowly forwards, while the legs move backward and upward to the surface. Recovery from this position to the upright may be achieved by laterally rotating onto the back and then effecting a forward recovery. But the head may also be strongly extended, the hips and knees flexed, and when the body is vertical the legs then extended and the body balanced precisely by the head in the upright position.

Lateral rotation

Lateral rotation occurs in two planes. In both of these, rotation takes place around the longitudinal axis. Vertically the swimmer is upright, and by movement of the head and arms is able to create a lateral or turning movement in the upright position. When lying in water the head, arms and legs, either singly or collectively, can be used to create lateral rotation around the longitudinal axis of the body.

An example of the kind of situation that can occur which demonstrates the need not only for rotational control but also for mental adjustment is where a child may be splashed when in the upright position. The action taken by the child is usually one of avoidance, and the head is turned to one side and at the same time sharply extended. The result is an immediate forward and upward movement of the legs with rotation to the side to which the head has been turned and consequent loss of balance.

Extremes of physical dimension

The extremes of physical dimension are arrived at when the body is curled up in its smallest shape — a 'ball' — and when the body is in its longest and thinnest shape — a 'stick'.

As a 'stick', the body, if standing vertically, is on a relatively small base and may be disturbed easily in any direction. If the stick is lying in water, it can again be easily disturbed and the movement which occurs is one of rotation around the longitudinal axis of the body. As a 'ball' the body balance is more stable and considerable effort is required to change the shape. Outside forces can disturb this shape, but simply cause it to rotate around its centre of buoyancy, and as these forces decrease or cease, the body returns to its floating position over the centre of buoyancy.

Thus it can be appreciated that the long thin shape (the 'stick') is the least stable, and the rounded shape (the 'ball') the most stable in water.

All early activities in water, therefore, should be carried out in shapes in which the body is collapsed down. Curled up as a 'ball' and keeping the body vertical by use of the head while performing activities such as 'bicycling' encourage head control, active movement and blowing in a stable position.

As ability in water improves, the child can undertake activities in a more extended position where the demand for a greater degree of control is required. Many activities involve a change of shape from one extreme to the other. For example 'Eggs for breakfast', 'Looby Loo', 'Rag dolls', 'The wheels of the bus', and so on (see pp. 102, 104, 114).

THE PHYSIOLOGICAL, THERAPEUTIC AND PSYCHOLOGICAL EFFECTS OF ACTIVITY IN WATER

The physiological and therapeutic effects of activity in water have been propounded by a number of authorities throughout the ages. In more recent years it has been suggested that the physiological effects of exercise combined with those effects brought about by the warmth of the water are one of the advantages of exercise in this medium. Such factors as the precise temperature of water, the duration of the treatment session, the type of exercise and the energy expended must be taken into account (Duffield, 1976).

The body possesses mechanisms for regulating its heat, and the maintenance of balance between the production of heat and heat loss requires fine adjustment (Chaffee and Lytle, 1980). A distinction has to be made between the core temperature of the body and that of the periphery (Janig, 1978), but under standard conditions body temperature in man remains remarkably constant. Fine diurnal changes in body temperature do occur throughout the day and vary for different parts of the body. Factors such as exercise, emotional disturbance and extremes of environmental temperatures may affect it, as well as age and sex (Downey, 1971). It is suggested by several authorities that the temperature of the skin is 33.3°C (92°F), though this may decrease in the most distal parts of the extremities (Finnerty and Corbitt, 1960; Bierman, 1963).

The body temperatures of children are less stable than those of adults. Warm and cold baths alter the temperature to a greater extent in the child than in the adult (Chaffee and Lytle, 1980). Therefore, when taking disabled children into water, a therapist must not only be aware of the degree of mobility of the children, but also of the precise temperature of the water. Programmes for children encourage active movement and swimming so the effects of too high or too low a water temperature should be understood. Children tend to be indefatigable and frequently want to continue with an activity for prolonged periods, especially one they are enjoying. Fatigue must be guarded against, particularly if the water temperature is high. If, on the other hand, the water temperature is lower and the child relatively immobile, heat loss from the child to the water must be closely monitored. The length of the period of water activity should, to some extent, be determined by these factors.

The effects of immersion in warm water are similar in adults and children and are related to body temperature, circulation and exercise, with variations allowing for size.

The therapeutic effects of exercise in water relate to:

(a) the relief of pain and muscle spasm,
(b) the maintenance or increase in range of motion of joints.
(c) the strengthening of weak muscles and an increase in their tolerance to exercise,
(d) the re-education of paralysed muscles,
(e) the improvement of the circulation,
(f) the encouragement of functional activities,
(g) the maintenance and improvement of balance, co-ordination and posture.

In addition, water provides the potential for exercise in three dimensions which cannot be achieved on land. There is also the possibility of considerable perceptual stimulation:

(a) visually,
(b) aurally,
(c) via the skin proprioceptors,
(d) by heat.

The eyes have to accommodate to the constantly changing levels of the water due to movement of the liquid and the poolside above the surface. When the ears are submerged there is greater pressure on them than there is in air. The skin reacts to different temperatures as well as appreciating the all-embracing effect of water on the body when immersed. Turbulent effects are initially felt by the skin, and when a limb is moving through the water the greatest appreciation of turbulence will be in the distal part.

Also, from a psychological standpoint there is much to recommend activity in water. Much of the information regarding the use of water in the treatment of mental illness throughout the ages came from disciplines such as sociology and anthropology. In more recent times the sedative effect of warm water and the value of swimming programmes for those persons affected by mental illness have been recognised (Wilson and Kasch, 1963; Kraus, 1973). From a humanistic point of view, the social and psychological significance that may be attached to the ability to swim is undoubtedly considerable.

The child who can swim and participate in other aquatic activities has gained a social asset. This ability places the child on an equal footing with other members of the family and with friends, whether able-bodied or disabled. The child can compete at a similar level. The ability to be independent in water, to achieve skills that may be difficult or impossible on land, can only have favourable and lasting psychological effects which boost confidence and morale, and these may well be carried over into life on land. For instance, a child handicapped with severe cerebral palsy learnt to swim at six years of age, a skill the nine-year-old brother had not acquired. This achievement not only increased the child's motivation and confidence, but had implications for the whole family who now perceived the child in a positive light.

Disabled children benefit from incentives and encouragement to improve stamina and techniques in the same manner as do able-bodied children. Once the skill of swimming has been learnt, the child can extend the activities, provided there are no medical problems which might make certain activities inappropriate. For example, the child who is competent in water could participate in survival techniques, take awards, gain skills in snorkelling or sub aqua diving and synchronised or competitive swimming. Other aquatic sports might include fishing, canoeing or perhaps sailing. Imagination and interest will suggest many other aquatic enjoyments which can be shared by the child and the family.

THERAPY AND RECREATION

A programme that combines both therapeutic and recreational aspects provides a more appropriate and enjoyable scheme for children, since hydrotherapy in the strict sense of remedial exercise may prove boring to them. It has been found that children, especially younger children, rarely respond directly to treatment techniques whether on land or in water (Reynell and Martin, 1965). However, water is an element that children enjoy from a very early age and from which they gain a variety of learning experiences. It is also a medium in which many disabled people achieve total independence and can compete with their able-bodied counterparts on equal terms. For those whose lives on land are spent in wheelchairs or walking with aids, independent walking in water can become a reality, in addition to all the rolling and tumbling activities which must be of delight to the performer who on land is so confined.

To get out of the wheelchair and to change one's wheelchair shape, to cast aside one's calipers and walking aids and find freedom of movement and independence brings about physical and psychological well-being which cannot be achieved to the same extent elsewhere or in any other activity.

If, then, both the therapeutic and recreational aspects of activity in water are based upon the same method, they become complementary to each other and provide a broader framework for the overall rehabilitation of the disabled child.

Traditionally, therapeutic techniques have tended to be used on a one-to-one basis, though the advantages of group work have not been ignored. In water a ratio of one therapist or instructor to each child provides a suitable situation, but group activity is beneficial. Therefore a group situation where each child is paired with an instructor provides the optimum situation for activity, motivation and progress.

Assessment

Assessment of the person referred for activity in water appears to have been largely ignored. However, Skinner and Thomson (1983) suggest that the therapist should undertake assessment both on land and in the water at the commencement of hydrotherapy treatment and at regular intervals throughout the treatment programme. A specific examination of such items as joint range, muscle power, balance and co-ordination, and gait is indicated, and examination of the person for contraindications to treatment, such as open wounds and skin lesions, especially tinea pedis, should be carried out prior to entry of the pool at every session.

Since the movements and abilities of the person on land will vary considerably from those same movements performed in water, it seems necessary to have a measure of assessment designed specifically for water activity. In water there is now the possibility of three-dimensional exercise; pain and muscle spasm may be eased by warmth and support of the water, and increased relaxation may well permit greater range of movement.

Therefore, assessment of the range of movement and muscle strength should be completed first on land and the same movements reassessed following entry into the water. A modified Oxford Scale of Muscle Power is provided for water, but this is limited to the assessment of muscles which retain little power but good range of movement (Skinner and Thomson, 1983). Matthews (1972) takes Foster's (1892) definition of muscle tone, which states that when a normal limb is moved passively there is a resistance to the movements. A satisfactory means of measuring muscle tone has yet to be developed on land. In water, where warmth and support tend to alter the tonal state, such measurement is even more complex. Smith (1979) suggests that muscle tone can be measured by the application of passive stretch and assessing the resistance offered by the muscle or muscles, although he does not clarify what form this assessment is to take. The therapist should assess tone on land by the method usually employed, whether this is by observation of movement, by handling, by observation of the effect of tonic reflexes or by any other method (Carr and Shepherd, 1980).

Reassessment should take place in water allowing for the effects of temperature, the supportive factor, and the anxiety level of the person in regard to water activity. This is a difficult task, which currently can only be undertaken on an individual basis but which may ultimately become easier if accurate recording of all the above factors is carried out serially.

It has already been shown in the text (see p. 20) that shape and density are of importance to water activity, so these factors must be studied in depth as they will influence the programme differently for each individual. This assessment is carried out by unobtrusively observing the person on land. When in water, the rotational effects caused by altered shape become evident, and the flotation of less dense body parts or the sinking of more dense parts is readily seen.

Therefore an accurate and detailed record of each person's general state and specific tone, range of movement and muscle power must be completed initially on land, then in water at successive intervals during treatment, and finally again on land at the completion of treatment. Though time consuming, this provides a clear impression of the person's response to treatment and, it is hoped, may lead to development of improved accuracy of assessment. It is essential as a basis for the rationale of hydrotherapy and evidence of its effectiveness in disease and disability.

If the person is to be taught independent dynamic movement in the water, it is important that the therapist assesses the person's ability to make a flat surface of the hands and feet. It is the large flat surfaces of the open hand, with adducted digits, and of the mobile feet that play an essential role in propelling the body through water (Counsilman, 1968). In some disabling conditions, the hands and feet are affected in such a way that it is not possible for a flat surface to be created — for example, the equinus deformity of the foot in muscular dystrophy, the flexor synergy of the hand in cases of hemiplegia, and the flexion of the metacarpophalangeal joints and ulnar deviation of the hand in the person suffering from rheumatoid arthritis.

A person who, prior to being referred for hydrotherapy, has had some experience of water will respond more satisfactorily to the demands in the medium than the person who, for one reason or another, is unfamiliar with water and is anxious or even afraid.

Time spent in explaining the reasons for treatment, the proposed programme and the value of exercise in water is therefore worthwhile. If shape and density have been observed carefully and the likely effects of water on the body analysed, it is possible to prepare the person mentally in advance for the activity.

Once in the medium, some time should be spent in encouraging the person to appreciate that water has weight, can be leant against and used as a force against which to work. Instruction should be given about breathing out both onto and into the water. Both these activities are best performed immediately on entry in the stable sitting position. When it is not possible for the person to flex the hips and knees sufficiently to obtain this posture with the shoulders beneath the surface, the adjustment to water and restoration of balance should be carried out in deeper water. If entry is by means of the steps or ramp, the therapist will be walking backwards supporting the person, whose hands are on the therapist's shoulders, at the waist. It is important to learn to lean from side to side and to step sideways, still in the basic sitting position. These activities should be followed by the person turning around to face away from the therapist, who now supports at the waist from behind. Instructions are given to the person to lean back slowly and let the head rest on the therapist's shoulder. The legs may be extended. Instructions are then given as to how the upright sitting posture may be regained.

When these points are understood, mental adjustment and balance restoration become easier, and assessment in water can be carried out more readily. This will also affect the person's ability to carry out the programme and respond in due course to greater demands for exercise.

When the disease or disability prevents entry by means of the steps or ramp and the person enters the pool over the side on a hoist, the method of developing mental adjustment and balance restoration will require modification. If the person is to be placed on a chair or plinth, the need for blowing out can be explained and encouraged. For the person who is sitting on a weighted chair to exercise, it is important that the therapist stresses the need for a forward action of the head to keep the body vertical. Most people will accept this if the reasons for it are carefully explained.

For those persons who, due to brain damage, are unable to respond or do so only very slowly, the methods of acquiring mental adjustment and balance restoration can be incorporated in the treatment programme.

FORMAT OF ASSESSMENT FOR HYDROTHERAPY

1. Aims of subjective assessment:
   - (a) to determine the person's present symptoms, their distribution and behaviour,
   - (b) to determine how the person's problem is related to total health and social conditions.

This can be achieved by reading the case notes or by taking a history. Points that have particular relevance to water activity can be noted. Can the person swim? If so, what is the level of swimming ability? Occasional recreation? Regular recreation? Competitive swimming? How long has the person been able to swim? When was the person last in the water?

2. Aims of objective assessment on land:
   - (a) to determine the degree of dysfunction,
   - (b) to determine the alterations in shape and density due to the disability in relation to the probable effect on the body in water,
   - (c) to provide specific assessment for presence of skin lesions and any contra-indications for hydrotherapy.
3. Aims of objective assessment in water:
   - (a) to determine the degree of dysfunction,
   - (b) to determine the effects of the altered shape and density on the body.

4. Analysis of findings and establishment of short- and long-term goals and the means by which these may be achieved.

5. Recording the assessment. Concise details of the assessment must be recorded and filed as a basis for evaluating progress. Detailed records of relevant assessments, reassessments and treatment programmes will permit continuity of treatment, progression of treatment, and provide valuable retrospective data for education and research (Parry, 1980).

Chapter 2

ACTIVITY IN WATER – WAYS AND MEANS

GENERAL PRINCIPLES

Activity in water is usually undertaken for one of two reasons: either to swim or to exercise.

As indicated earlier in the text (see p. 30), pure exercise may prove boring to children, and games and activities that are fun are more likely to develop the skills required and achieve the aims of the programme. The ingenuity and imagination of the therapist are taxed in devising those activities which will meet the objectives of exercises in water and promote the learning of needed skills. Additionally, programmes must be planned which successfully combine therapeutic and recreational benefits.

Safety, discipline and bathside management

The therapist must, at all times, be aware of the attendant risks both in and out of the water, and be able to deal with any emergency should it arise. Emergencies are rare occurrences but can be further minimised by attention to factors such as having:

(a) a thorough knowledge of the disabilities,
(b) an understanding of the physiological effects of exercise in water,
(c) an ability to carry out resuscitation techniques.
(d) basic rules for bathside and water management.

Basic rules for bathside management relate to the prohibition of running on the poolside, and every care should be taken when children using crutches or walking aids fitted with rubber ferrules are moving about in the changing rooms or on the poolside, which may be wet.

A safety drill to be observed in an emergency should be planned and practised at regular intervals. All concerned with the water activity should understand the signal and what action is required. Certain precautions in relation to particular disabilities are provided in the chapters concerned with those various disabilities.

Child–therapist relationship

A child's progress in activity in water is in some measure directly attributable to the child–therapist relationship. It is important, therefore, that certain aspects of this are understood.

For many children, the initial introduction to water is a matter of anxiety. A therapist who is unsure of the properties and characteristics of water, who lacks stability and balance and is reluctant to submerge is unlikely to be able to give reassurance. Poor handling and holds can also mar the experience for the child. Thus precise holds, careful handling and the ability of the therapist to cope with the body are of first concern in establishing a good water situation.

Ingenuity and imagination in developing games and activities, the use of rhythm, the voice and other factors described in the development of games (see p. 61) assist in easing a tense situation.

It is possible for a child to become too dependent on one therapist, and in most instances this should be avoided. A change of therapist can be readily achieved in a group where the activities require the children to move from one therapist to the next. In certain conditions, however, it can be advisable for the same therapist to continue working with one child. For instance, where a problem of communication exists and the therapist has established a rapport and an effective means of communicating with the child, the relationship should be maintained throughout treatments.

Achievement should always be acknowledged. The acquisition of a skill, whether blowing a bubble or retrieving a submerged object, needs to be recognised and praised if performed correctly. In this way a happy child–therapist relationship is also developed.

INDIVIDUAL AND GROUP ACTIVITIES

Advantages

The opportunity to work both individually and in groups provides the optimal situation for the child.

Many of the activities described in the text can be taught individually as well as in a group situation, and where a precise action requires particular attention and training, individual work may be used to advantage. However, on a one-to-one child–therapist relationship within a group such training may also be achieved. At the same time the child benefits from the other advantages of working with others and is provided with the opportunity to acquire the required skills without undue attention being drawn to their absence.

Grouping

When planning a group, ability in the water is the major concern and the ages of the children a secondary consideration. The size, depth and shape of the pool must be taken into account together with the ease with which the therapist can control the group.

The ability of the various children in the water should be fairly similar, but some disparity allows for the development of incentives.

A group is disadvantaged when all the children within it have the same disability. Progress is slowed, incentives are not developed and motivation is harder to establish. Socialisation is diminished when the children are not given the opportunity of meeting others outside their usual environment.

Too great a discrepancy in age between the children in the group tends to disadvantage the younger and smaller children, particularly during more energetic activities.

The numbr considered most suitable for a group is six or eight swimmers. But the size of the group will to some extent be determined by the size, depth and shape of the pool. It has to be remembered that six or eight children require the presence of six to eight therapists and helpers, and the size and shape may not allow for 12 to 16 persons. It requires considerable ability to control a group of this size in activities, especially to raise the voice above the general noise level concomitant with such group activity and to maintain the group as a cohesive unit.

Group function

Groups provide stimulation, motivation and a social community. Many disabled children have, of necessity, a considerable amount of attention and treatment and are set apart in some respects, isolated and insulated from experiences and activities able-bodied children develop naturally and take for granted. In a group this situation is altered. The disabled child is no longer special, but part of a unit involved in activities with others. The child may not be able to participate fully at first, but is stimulated by the ability and appreciation of other group members; thus incentives are provided and increased participation developed. Motivation and socialisation are valuable elements of group work, and the ability to concentrate and work for longer periods of time is enhanced by the group situation.

Groups provide a secure environment in which to perform the activities and such security can be developed further by the ability and personality of the group leader and by advanced planning. A happy atmosphere is beneficial to all and provides the appropriate conditions for achieving therapeutic and recreational aims.

Water activity for the young child, 0–4 years

Infants and young children will have experienced water in the bath, but the transition to a pool and a much larger expanse of water may, of course, give rise to anxiety.

The teaching of swimming is considered by

many authorities to be most appropriately begun when the child is about four years of age. At this time the ability to reason is developing (Gesell and Bates, 1976) and the child is becoming ready for school. However, this does not imply that children under four years of age should not be taken into water. Water-familiarisation programmes have been developed by many people as a preparation for learning to swim (Elkington, 1978; Blanksby and Roberts, 1981; Bullock, 1982). Holt (1975, p. 13), discussing Piaget's contribution to child development, says that the child's 'sensori-motor stage has equipped him to explore further as he does in constant play'.

Play and games have a major role in a child's development (see p. 60). From the early days of life the infant interacts with and relates to the parents or care-giver, observing and imitating behaviour and actions. Thus the provision of suitable opportunities and equipment is an essential part of the caring environment for young children whether able-bodied or disabled. In fact, group activity for this 0–4-year age group has been found valuable for both parent and child. But an essential ingredient when considering water activity for young children is security. Security is found in the parent's arms and in contact with the body. It is found in the sensation of the fluid environment, experienced prenatally, and now re-experienced in the warmth of the water. Security is further enhanced if initially the child is kept mainly in the upright position. The hold should be at the child's waist level, and any movement of the head with a resultant swinging action of the feet can be controlled by the parent. A watchful parent can help the child appreciate the effect of movement of the head on the body by allowing the body and feet to swing in one direction or the other when the head is taken forwards or backwards, and facilitating return to the upright position. In this way the need for head control is instilled in the child from the very beginning.

In addition to providing security within the parent's arms, colourful floating toys and objects which interest and attract the child should be used not only to break up the surface of the water and lessen the apparent vastness of the expanse, but as a means of introducing activity.

Although children under the age of 12 months are unlikely to be able to blow regularly into or onto the water, imitation of playful vocal sounds by adults occurs from approximately 9 months of age. The parent should demonstrate blowing in a noisy fashion to attract the child's attention and encourage imitation. In this way emphasis is laid on the essential skill of breathing control. Toys that can be blown over the surface of the water prove helpful, and, in bringing the head towards the object, head control is improved. Where a child has poor eye contact, focusing on the parent's vocal blowing sound helps gain better eye contact and head control.

Time spent in explaining to parents certain points about water activity is never wasted. If parents understand the reasons for particular holds and why certain actions are encouraged, the responses of the children will be enhanced.

Explanations need to cover the following points.

1. Why the body of a young child floats.
2. Why the child under five months of age 'swims'.
3. The importance of breathing control.
4. The importance of a forward head movement towards the water.
5. The importance of correct holding and gradual disengagement.
6. The need for control of the limbs.
7. The need for learning rotational skills.
8. The need for active movement.

The majority of these points have been discussed elsewhere in this book (see, for example, 'Introduction'), but the author believes it is of such importance that parents are made aware of these facts that further space is devoted here to the explanations which accompany the rules.

Why the body of a young child floats

The relative density of the body of the infant and young child is approximately 0.86 and therefore in the ratio of 0.86 of the child to the relative density of water which is 1, the child will float. Flotation may occur in both the face upwards or face downwards position, but the latter is totally unsafe. The child may in some instances instinctively rotate the body from the face-down position, but is unlikely to do this automatically until able to reason. Therefore the importance of total vigilance at all times when a child is near or in water becomes evident.

Why the child under five months of age 'swims'

Several authorities describe reflex swimming movements seen in children as young as 11 days old when held in or over water (Cratty, 1979). Since a child of this age has no head control, the head must be supported otherwise the face will submerge. The movements are more rhythmical than the crawling pattern which results from eliciting the crawling reflex. The reflex swimming movements have usually disappeared by five months of age

Such reflex action should not be interpreted as proof that the child is swimming and, by implication, that the child is therefore able to swim enough to prevent drowning should a fall into water occur.

The importance of breathing control

The importance of breathing control has been discussed earlier in the text but is reinforced by the manner in which blowing bubbles forms part of water-familiarisation programmes (Elkington,

1978; Bullock 1982). The ability to control respiration is vital when learning different swimming strokes (Counsilman 1968; Elkington 1978; Blanksby and Roberts, 1981). Blowing bubbles forces the water away from the nose and mouth and helps avoid taking water into the lungs or into the eustachian tubes and facial sinuses.

Many authors (for example Bullock, 1982) conclude that blowing bubbles is of first importance and can be regarded as an exercise leading to progressive submergence. The value of personal demonstration by the parent to the child is stressed and can be started at home in the bath. Appropriate toys such as fish, ducks, boats and balls that can be blown across the surface of the water may prove useful. Pouring water from teapots and jugs into other containers may be valuable in teaching manipulative skills on land. However, such items are not appropriate in a pool where a child might be encouraged to drink from them.

The importance of a forward head movement towards the water

Two points need to be understood in relation to forward head movement. First, if the head is extended when submerging, water may be forced up the nose if the child is not blowing. The infant and young child who has not established a regular blowing action is at great risk, especially if a fall into water occurs or the child is tossed into the air and allowed to submerge. A study of anatomy of the head and neck shows how the meninges of the brain dip down through the cribriform plate at the base of the skull just above the upper part of the nose. Water forced up the nose may come into contact with the meninges — a possible site for infection (see Appendix). Water forced up the nose may also produce infections of the eustachian tubes and in the middle ear. In addition, in the neonate and infant the tympanic membrane is close to the surface, the growth of the external auditory meatus gradually affording protection as the child develops. This, however, is not complete until the fifth year of life (*Gray's Anatomy*, 1973). Since pressure on the ears is greater in water than in air, prolonged underwater activity should be avoided in the young child (see Appendix).

The second point relates to head posture and balance. If the head is brought forward, vertical balance can be maintained and such action is important for head control.

The importance of correct holding and gradual disengagement

The manner in which this point can best be explained to parents is by using the parents as models. The parent is encouraged to lie back on the therapist's hands using the backing hold described (see p. 55). The parent is then instructed how to lie back and recover forward as for vertical rotation (see p. 26). No physical assistance is given by the therapist in the creation of the movement, and after several repetitions the therapist transfers the supporting hands to the parent's scapulae. The lying back and recovering actions are repeated. In addition to the lesser degree of control with this hold, the altered position of the body in the supine lying position can be appreciated. When the hold is at the scapula level and the body is lying supine, there is a marked tendency for the feet to drop and the body to lie at an angle of 40°–45°. The parent then takes the therapist's place and acts as the support for the therapist in order that the parent realises the difference between the two holds in the degree to which control of the supported body is achieved.

Disengagement has been discussed (see p. 39), but it is important to ensure that the parents understand the need for gradual disengagement as the child acquires a skill.

The need for control of the limbs

Control of the limbs is important in water not only for swimming with rhythmical movements of the arms and legs, but also in its relation to meta-centric effects (see p. 16). Parents come to a quicker understanding of this point if encouraged to experience the effects. This can be demonstrated by walking from shallow to deep water with hands clasped behind the back. When submerged in water up to the nostrils, the parents turn round and try to walk back to the shallow end of the pool. This is virtually impossible until the arms are raised above the head. Gravitational effects will to some extent then overcome buoyancy effects. The heels will drop to the floor of the pool and, with generation of a frictional force between the soles of the feet and the floor, it becomes possible to walk to shallow water. Alternatively, the parents can be asked to sit with the angles, knees and hips at right-angles, the feet placed hip width apart and flat on the floor of the pool. The shoulders should be just below the surface of the water. One or both arms can be raised above the surface and held elevated whilst gravitational effects are appreciated. Another way in which meta-centric effects can be experienced is by lying supine in the water in a 'stick' shape and raising one arm above the water towards the ceiling. The body will roll to the side on which the arm is lifted, rotating until it finds its point of balance face down in the water. If both arms are raised simultaneously, the body will sink first and then roll to whichever side is denser or shorter.

From these experiences, the need to keep as much of the body as possible in the water becomes evident, and so the need for control of the limbs is obvious.

The need for rotational control

It will be recalled that two planes of rotation are

possible in water. Most parents appreciate the necessity for being able to recover to a safe breathing position, but how to achieve this without the data points or points of resistance present on land needs to be explained and demonstrated. When taking young children into water, it is frequently found that rotation occurs as part of the normal pattern of development. The parent should be encouraged to allow both vertical and lateral rotation to occur, facilitated and/or controlled by them.

The need for active movement

The reasons for active rather than passive movement are explained to the parents. A certain amount of passive movement may be necessary to show the child the action required, but it should cease immediately the child achieves the movement or attempts it.

A programme for the infant or young child includes activities such as blowing bubbles, trying to blow toys across the surface of the water, riding a bicycle, swinging as in the primary activity in 'Bells', splashing with fingers, hands, arms and legs, making waves and lifting the water through the fingers and also with a cupped hand.

Objects lighter than water can also be pushed under the surface and released so the child can watch them rise again. In this way the effect of buoyancy is introduced at an early stage and can be related to the effect on the human body later. With this age group and with those children whose head control and eye contact are poor, the parents are encouraged to dance to music in the water with the children held in the arms facing them and in contact with the body, thus providing security, tactile stimulation, body awareness and head control. In addition, the music provides a means of encouraging an appreciation of rhythm.

As the children progress, extension of the programme is made by using the activities and games for older children and progressing from the primary to the advanced aspect of each.

ACTIVITIES AND GAMES

Entry and exit

There is a marked tendency amongst those working with disabled persons to use hoists, ramps and special wheeled chairs to get disabled swimmers into and out of the water. In the author's experience there is little need for this, as in most cases even the most severely disabled can be got into water over the side of the pool. All mechanical means of entry and exit place the disabled in an invidious position: already set apart by disability, a further handicap is placed upon them. Instead, the disabled should be enabled to participate in as normal a manner as possible so that integration, participation and socialisation may become a reality. The earlier these aspects can be incorporated into water activity, the greater becomes the realisation of these goals.

A method of entry and exit should be devised and developed so that in due course the disabled child enters and leaves the water independently. If the integration of disabled persons — whether children or adults — into normal life is desired, this is essential.

While appreciating that a few extremely disabled children may not achieve such independence, the author suggests that the following methods of entry and exit offer an appropriate means of help in the majority of instances. The most severely disabled may not progress beyond the first or second stages of entry and may never achieve exit over the side without assistance. But every effort should be made to try to obtain the greatest possible independence. These methods of entry and exit can be learned by anyone, and thus attendance at local swimming clubs and pools need not be a barrier. The able-bodied members can assist in entry and exit, be helped to understand the nature of the disability and how to overcome the problems relating to it. It is reiterated that it is unfortunate that the emphasis in the literature is on dependence on mechanical aids rather than on encouraging the use of the mobility and motivation of the disabled person.

Focal points

Certain other factors, in addition to those discussed in the 'Introduction', have to be taken into account when first introducing children to water.

Even a small expanse of water can seem vast and frightening to a child. To avoid distress, the therapist should always be in the water waiting at the side, at an appropriate depth, to receive the child. The therapist then acts as a focal point when the child is placed in the sitting position on the poolside prior to entry. The therapist and child can communicate easily, and encouragement and instructions can be given to the child, as well as physical support. If the distance from the poolside to water surface appears too great from the perspective of the child, the presence of the therapist in the water can help to reduce this effect.

Entry

On entering the water the therapist should move gently and avoid splashing. By ducking down, getting wet and blowing bubbles, it can be demonstrated to the child that water is a pleasant and enjoyable medium. Even if the water is cooler than desired or expected, the child must not become aware of this fact. Every child is probably anxious about entering water, so it is important that the therapist shows no anxiety and that the water should not be cold (Reid, 1975).

The therapist may work across a corner or use the shortest distance of the pool to provide a focal point, and the surface of the water will be broken up by a selection of interesting toys. In these ways, anxiety is lessened and active participation encouraged.

The sitting position has already been shown to be a stable one in water and thus a 'sitting' entry from the side ensures the child enters from a position of stability (Fig. 10).

The child is encouraged to reach forward and place the hands on the therapist's shoulders. The therapist's hands are placed on the child's back just below the lower border of the scapulae. The stance adopted by the therapist is important. Step standing with the toes of the forward foot touching the wall ensures that a step backwards can be taken as the child enters the water. Talking to the child, encouraging a blowing action as the entry is made, reduces anxiety and assists in bringing the head forward towards the water. At no time should the child be allowed to place the feet against the wall or on a rail, nor extend the head and trunk as entry is made. To ensure that this does not occur, the therapist can exert pressure through the hands, bringing the child into the pool with a forward action.

Once the child is in the water, it is advantageous to commence activity immediately, thus distracting the child's thoughts and avoiding anxiety about being in water, or about the water temperature.

Fig. 10 *Sitting entry.*

The best activities are those that keep the child in a stable 'ball' shape, such as 'Bicycles' or 'Bells' performed individually, or a jumping action which allows partial extension into a 'stick' shape. In all cases it is the 'blowing' that is important and this should be introduced rhythmically from the start.

As the child progresses and is more confident of entry, a 'hands on hands' hold is employed (Fig. 11). The therapist's stance is similar to that for the previous hold, but the child now places the hands palm downwards on the upturned hands of the therapist. Later a gap can be left between the child's hands and those of the therapist. The latter picks up the child's hands as the water is entered (Fig. 12).

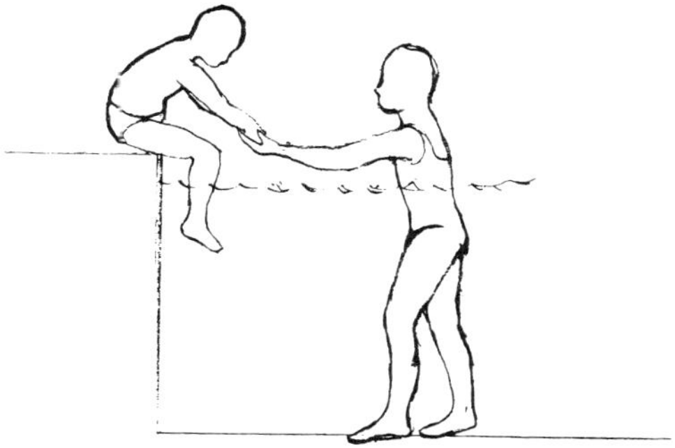

Fig. 11 *Entry—hands on hands.*

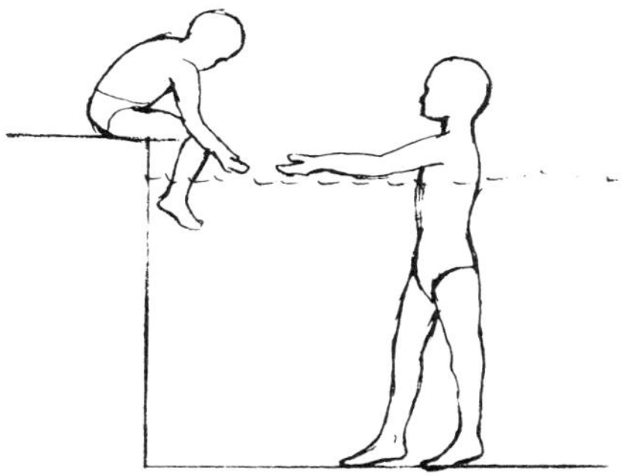

Fig. 12 *Sitting entry—a gap between the child's hands and those of the therapist.*

The final progression is independent entry, first using forward rotation (Fig. 13), and then lateral rotation to a supine lying position (Fig. 14) and

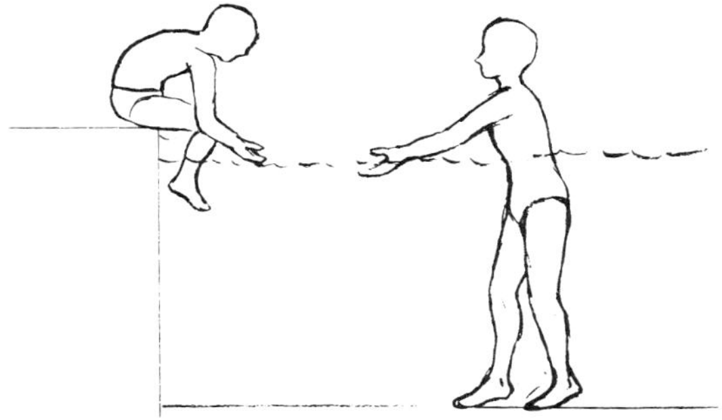

Fig. 13 *Independent entry—falling forward.*

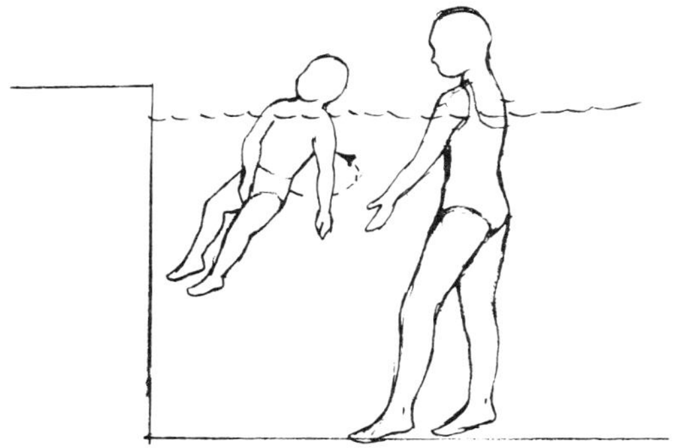

Fig. 14 *Independent entry—lateral rotation on to the back.*

either recovering forwards to the side of the pool or swimming away.

Forward and lateral rotational movements may be combined to produce another and more advanced method of entry (Fig. 15). The child sits on the poolside and the therapist takes up a stance in the lunge position diagonally to one side of the child. The child's arm on the side opposite to that on which the therapist is standing is taken by the therapist using the arm closest to the child. A hold is made by the therapist's cupped hand placed under the upper arm of the child. The latter then places the hand on the therapist's arm. Where necessary, support may be given to the child's legs by the therapist's outer arm, or it may be held just below the surface of the water ready to provide support under the back as the child enters the water. The child's arm which is not being held must be placed on the lap. To obtain combined rotation it is essential that the child is instructed to look at the therapist throughout the entry. As the child's body comes forwards and rotates onto the back, the therapist sweeps the child out into the water ensuring that the legs do not come into contact with the wall of the pool.

Fig. 15 *Entry—combined rotation.*

The important points to watch in all entries described are:

(a) that the child comes forward towards the water and at no time extends the head and trunk,

(b) that the child always blows as the forward movement towards the water occurs so that no water enters the mouth,

(c) that the child's feet hang free of the bar and side of the pool.

It is useful for the child to be talking or singing a song or nursery rhyme when entering. Air is being expelled and water is less likely to enter the mouth. It is also a means of distracting the child, especially if it is a favourite song.

The above entries may have to be modified for some children, but it must be borne in mind that the aim is a method of entry and exit that the child can ultimately use independently.

Method of entry for the severely disabled

If the disabled child can sit, even though requiring support, the following method of entry may be used. The therapist is in the water standing in a lunge position. The forward foot is close to the wall and bears the body weight. The child is brought towards the edge of the pool by a rocking movement in which the body weight is transferred from side to side. As the body weight is taken off one hip, so the therapist facilitates a forward movement of that hip and leg. Once the child is close to the edge, the knees are placed high up on the therapist's shoulders on either side of the head. The child is instructed to place the hands over and behind the therapist's shoulders so that they are over the latter's scapulae. The child is further instructed to lean the head to one side of the therapist's head, but moving in the opposite direction (Fig. 16). To achieve entry the therapist continues the gentle rocking movement until the child's hips are clear of the wall. Still supporting the child at the hips, the body is lifted and lowered into the water as the therapist steps back, bending the knees to permit entry as soon as possible so that water takes most of the body weight. Only momentarily does the therapist have the full weight of the child on the shoulders and, as this force is directly over the therapist's centre of gravity, the weight is translated correctly through the body and entry achieved with a minimum of effort.

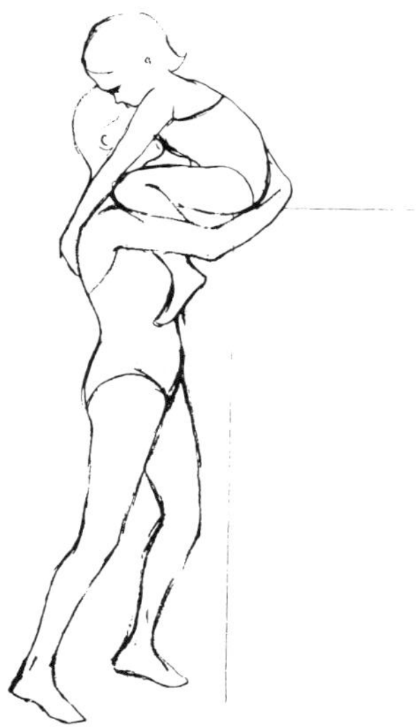

Fig. 16 *Entry for a severely disabled person.*

Exit

Many disabled children *can* exit from the water over the side, and this should be encouraged for reasons of independence. The basis of the exit described below is connected with the theory of boundary layer (Shapiro, 1961).

The child places, or is assisted to place, both hands on the wall (Fig. 17a). The therapist holds the child on the lateral sides of the thighs just below the greater trochanter of the femur and helps the child

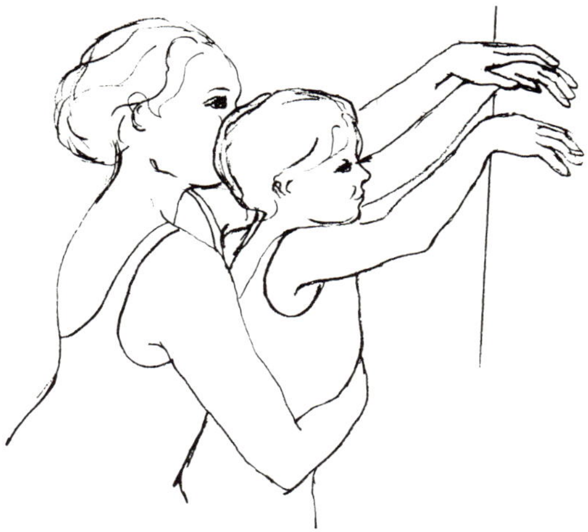

Fig. 17a *Exit over the side — hands on the poolside.*

Fig. 17b *Exit over the side — assisted on to the poolside, the child's legs are kept close to the wall.*

to move onto the wall so that the body is lying on it. The hips remain flexed, thus keeping the legs close against the poolside (Fig. 17b). This is an important point for the child to appreciate, for if the hips and legs are extended and trailing in the water and if the water is flowing swiftly or is turbulent, the child could be dragged back into the pool.

The therapist then assists the child to lift the legs quickly high and clear of the water as the child works forward pushing on the hands (Fig. 17c). Once the hips are over the pool edge, a rolling action is created by the child (Fig. 17d). This can be facilitated by the therapist crossing the child's legs at the ankles and assisting sitting up through rotation by taking the child's arm across the body (Fig. 17e).

Any mobility the child has should be used increasingly until the exit can be made independently.

Severely disabled children with poor head control and little use of their arms can use this form of exit. However, more assistance is needed, and another person on the bathside, if present, can

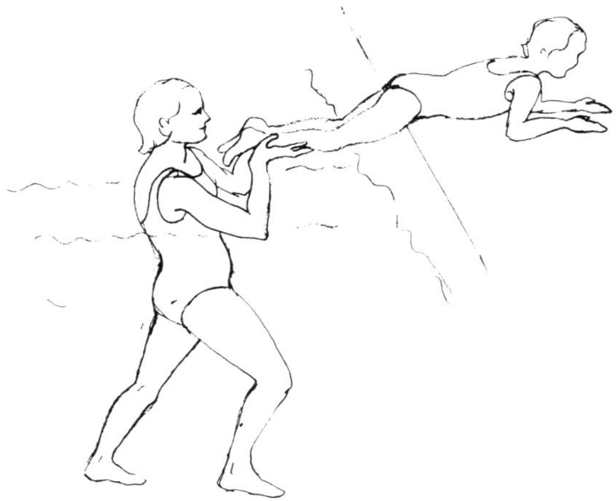

Fig. 17c *Exit over the side — the legs lifted together, high and clear of the water.*

Fig. 17d *Exit over the side — the child is helped to wriggle forwards over the poolside and then to rotate.*

control the head and arms. In the case of smaller children, the therapist can manage to control and assist them alone.

The modification of this exit for the child with spinal bifida is described on p. 205.

Exit for the severely disabled child

A few severely disabled children may not be able to exit over the side of the pool in the manner described and require lifting from the water. Two or three people, depending on the size and weight of

Fig. 17e *Exit over the side — assistance is given to sitting up with rotation.*

the child to be lifted, will be required in the water and one on the bathside. Small children may be lifted out by one person but it is still essential to have another person on the bathside.

The lifters stand in a line, shoulder to shoulder, facing the poolside and supporting the child on extended arms with the palms facing downwards. If three lifters are used, the person at the child's head and upper trunk places one arm under the neck, the other under the back at the lower angle of the scapulae. The lifter in the middle places one arm under the back against the first lifter's arm and the other under the child's thighs. The third lifter places one arm under the thighs against the previous lifter's arm and the other under the ankles.

It is important that the child remains still, with the hands crossed at the wrists and resting as low on the body as possible. Working in unison, standing in a lunge position, all with the same leg forward, the command 'up' is given and the child's weight is thus taken onto the extended arms of the lifters. The weight is taken off by the water as the lifters lower the arms. This up–down action is repeated three times, and on the fourth up the lifters step forward placing the child on to the poolside, still on the arms. The lifter controlling the head and upper trunk starts to move the shoulders away and upwards from the poolside, the assistant on the poolside taking over to facilitate sitting up. The lifter controlling the pelvis rotates the hips towards the water, at the same time facilitating the sitting position. The legs and feet are moved towards the water by the third lifter, so that the final outcome is a supported sitting position for the child on the poolside with the feet in the water.

When using this lift the following points must be remembered.

1. The shape and density of the body to be lifted and the appropriate positioning of the lifters according to ability and strength to lift along the child's body. For example, where the hips and pelvis of the child are the largest and densest part of the body, the strongest person should be the middle of the three lifters in the water.

2. All lifters should have a lunging stance with the same foot forward.

3. The arms supporting the child should be palms downwards and extended. Fingers should be extended, with the fingertips just touching the side of the pool. Fingers should not be holding the bar or any other projection.

4. Lifting should be done in unison, therefore one person should issue the commands.

5. The child being lifted should remain still and the arms kept on top on the body. Where the arms cannot be placed as suggested due to the disability, the assistant on the bathside must control the arm closest to the side of the pool and ensure that no friction occurs as the body is lifted on to the side.

Suggested songs and rhymes for entry

Many songs and rhymes are suitable for entry into the water. A few suggestions are given here.

'Jack and Jill'
'Humpty Dumpty'
'Green bottles'
Counting.

In a group which consists of boys and girls, 'Jack and Jill' provides a good rhyme for entering the water. At the words 'Jack fell down', the boys enter the water, and the girls follow at the words 'Jill came tumbling after'. The next two verses of this nursery rhyme can be utilised to practise jumping and blowing, and the group can move into the formation required for the next activity.

'Humpty Dumpty' can be used individually or in a group situation. It may be advantageous when first introducing a child to water to substitute the word 'blow' for 'fall'. The remaining lines of the rhyme may be used to practise jumping and blowing.

Using the song 'Green bottles', the number of bottles should match the number of children and all the bottles can 'fall' into the water together.

When using counting, each child is given a number and enters the water when the number is called. This is a useful method of entry in a group where some children are happier to enter the water than others.

Whatever rhyme or song is used, the purpose is to encourage a forward entry freely and confidently. The therapist is concerned that a correct forward action and blowing are developed.

Some swimmers prefer to enter and exit from the water by the steps or ramp when these form part of the construction of the pool. This preference can be allowed, but the therapist should bear in mind that the swimmer, at some point in the future, may participate in aquatic activities in a pool or other place where steps and ramps are not available. If entry is carried out in this manner, the therapist should walk backwards in front of the swimmer and provide any appropriate assistance. When the exit is made by means of the steps or ramp, the therapist should be behind the swimmer providing support if necessary, and should not leave the person until safely on the bathside.

Principles of holding

The manner in which the child is held contributes to confidence and to the degree of activity and progress that is achieved. It is essential that the holds are accurate, and constant observation is necessary in order that alterations and modifications of the holds are made commensurate with the child's progress in the skills being taught. Appropriate holds also provide the child with tactile stimulation and improve body awareness (Campbell, 1978). The points of resistance against which the human being works on land are removed in water. The new point of resistance — or datum point — is the centre of balance of the body. This is just below waist level and therefore holds should be made at or around this point. Effective control of the body is then obtained and a feeling of security imparted. Whatever position the therapist takes up in relation to the child, this principle applies.

The amount of support given should be kept to a minimum so that maximum control of the body can be achieved. Holds should be relaxed and gripping avoided. Gripping may produce discomfort, increase tension and induce a change in shape with consequent alteration in balance, however small. The stability of the therapist providing support to the child is vital. Whatever hold is used, the therapist should have a wide stance, be well balanced and keep the shoulders at water level. The stability of this stance provides the necessary stable support for the child and also ensures that work takes place at the level of the child in the water. Thus the balance is not disturbed and communication can take place easily.

In cases of severe disabilities where marked alterations in shape and/or density are present, or where one side of the body is considerably more affected than the other, modifications of holds may need to be made. It should be borne in mind,

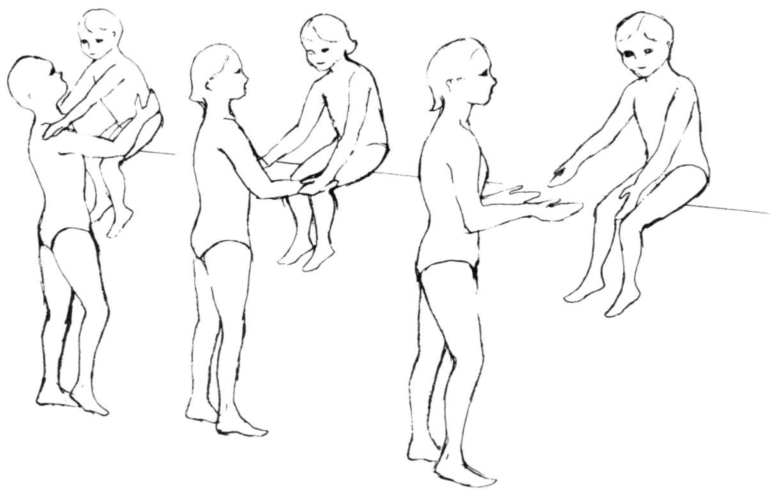

Fig. 18 *Group entry — showing three different holds.*

however, that the ultimate aim is the independence of the child, and modifications that have been made should be reduced and ideal holds slowly introduced so that eventually the removal of all support becomes possible.

It is inadvisable to hold the child's head. Since the head controls the body and feet, holding of the head by another person removes the ability to produce that control independently. It has also been found to be alarming to children to be held by the head and towed through the water. This could well occur because the feeling of control over the body by movement of the head is lost. An exception to this is described under cerebral palsy (see p. 215).

Holds — facing

Since entry is made with child and therapist facing each other, it is simple to commence activities in this position.

If entry is made with the child's hands on the therapist's shoulders (see p. 43), the first face-to-face engagement is achieved.

1. The child faces the therapist, whose hands are placed on the child's waist, fingers pointing away. The child is then encouraged to extend the arms and place the hands on the therapist's shoulders (Fig. 19).

Modifications of this hold may be required when the child is unable to extend the arms. Support is then given under the axilla, allowing the child's

Fig. 19 *First facing hold.*

arms to rest on those of the therapist.

2. 'Hands on hands' hold is achieved by the child placing the open hands palm down on the upturned palms of the therapist (Fig. 20). The arms should be extended as much as possible. This hold may be progressed to a one-hand or fingertip hold.

If work is taking place in a water depth where the child cannot touch the bottom of the pool, or if the child is small and a base is required, this can be provided by the thighs of the therapist.

3. If a child has marked hypotonicity, the following hold, which gives adequate support and allows participation in many activities, can be used. The child's legs straddle those of the therapist who is in the stable 'sitting' position. The therapist's

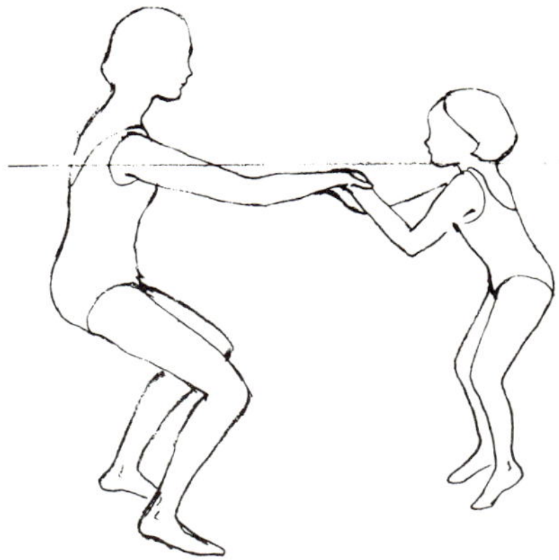

Fig. 20 *Facing hold — hands on hands.*

Fig. 21a *Holding a severely hypotonic child.*

hands support the lumbar spine and the neck and lower part of the occiput of the child, the arms passing under the child's arms which can float free, be placed on the therapist's shoulders or, when taking part in an activity in a circle, can be held by the persons on either side (Fig. 21a). When using this hold in a group activity, the therapist will work with the back into the circle so that the child can observe the activity of the rest of the group and be part of it.

When some degree of head control is present, this hold may be modified to support the child between the scapulae with one hand, or with both hands, one behind each scapula (Fig. 21b).

Holds — backing

The therapist works from behind the child in the ensuing holds.

1. When the child has a severe disability the following hold may be employed. The child sits on the therapist's thighs, with arms forward and supported on those of the therapist. The child's elbows are outside the therapist's and the hands are on top of the therapist's hands (Fig. 22). The progression for this hold is the placing of the child's elbows inside the therapist's arms. At times it is necessary for the therapist to hold the child's forearms rather than hands to facilitate extension of the arms for-

Fig. 21b *Modification of the hold for a hypotonic child.*

Fig. 22 *Hold for a severely disabled child.*

Fig. 23 *Backing hold—vertical position.*

ward and maintain them close to the surface. Further progressions for the severely disabled child follow the lines of the backing holds for other children.

2. When requiring stabilisation in the vertical position, the therapist supports the child at the waist, fingers pointing forwards (Fig. 23).

3. When moving from the vertical position to horizontal supine lying, the therapist supports the child in the upright position with the heel of the hands in the child's waist, the fingers pointing downwards over the child's buttocks. The child can then lie back on the flat hands of the therapist

(Fig. 24). To attain the vertical position the child creates a forward recovery and the supporting hands do not alter their position. Should the child overbalance forwards in trying to gain the upright position, the therapist can readily move the fingers to a forward-pointing position and steady the child with the fingertips over the anterior superior iliac spines.

4. For activities where a line with alternate swimmer and therapist (one behind the other) is required, support is given by the therapist in one of two ways.

(a) Forward under the swimmer's arms around the waist of the therapist in front. Where the swimmer has difficulty bringing the arms forward, the therapist may hold the swimmer's arms and take them forward around the waist of the therapist ahead,

(b) Around the waist of the swimmer, who holds around the waist of the therapist in front.

Fig. 24 *Backing hold—horizontal position.*

In due course, as ability increases, the swimmer may be placed behind the therapist. At all times safety of hold and the effects of turbulence must be understood and appreciated.

The bicycle hold has several progressions. With severely disabled children the backing hold first described (see p. 53) can be used. As progress is made the normal cycle holds are employed.

1. The child faces away from the therapist, who supports the child's forearms with the arms held outside those of the child (Fig. 25a).

2. To decrease support, the child places the palms downwards on the therapist's clenched fists, the elbows being inside the therapist's arms (Fig. 25b).

3. The therapist's extended thumbs give less support to the child who clasps them. Again, the child's elbows are inside the therapist's arms (Fig. 25c).

4. During the development of lateral rotational control in the vertical position, certain activities require a hold that provides a degree of independence but prevents the loss of balance. The therapist's arms form a circle around the swimmer's body under the arms. This allows the swimmer freedom

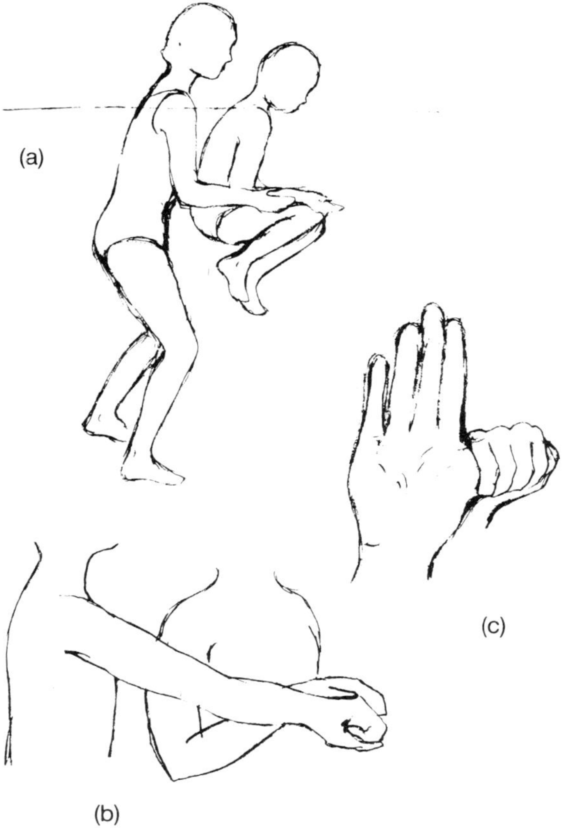

Fig. 25 (a) *Bicycle hold.* (b) *Modification of bicycle hold — clenched fist.* (c) *Modification of bicycle hold — thumb hold.*

of movement within the encircling arms. Furthermore, the swimmer is able to use the therapist's arms as a support and a means of facilitating lateral rotation (see Fig. 31, p. 59).

Holds for line or circle activities

1. An across the back hold is formed by the therapist placing the child to one side and taking the arm nearest to the child, across the child's back at waist level. The therapist's hand is placed over the front of the pelvis just above the hip joint and the child held in contact with the therapist's body (Fig. 26). This hold is used when the child's disability prevents the use of an arm for holding. When both

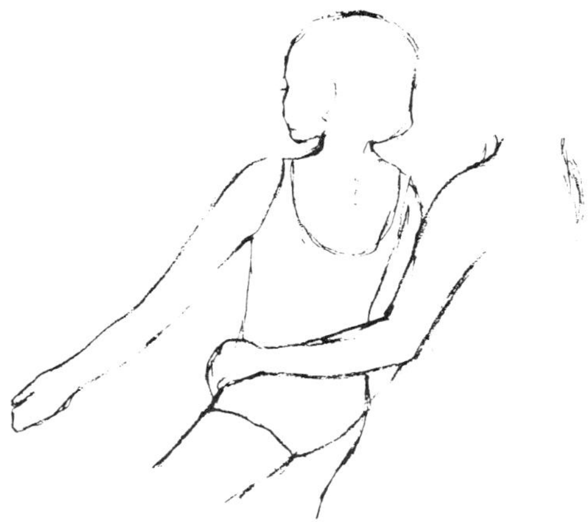

Fig. 26 *Across the back hold.*

arms are involved the therapists on either side of the child embrace the child in the same manner. The forearms and elbows can be used to maintain the required position of the child's body in an activity and facilitate or control swinging actions.

2. A short arm hold is one in which the upper arm of the therapist is placed under that of the child and the latter's forearm rests in the therapist's upturned hand. This avoids the intertwining of fingers which can lead to gripping, discomfort and tension. The correct position of the child, and forward and backward swinging actions, can be facilitated and controlled by the therapist's hands and forearms (Fig. 27).

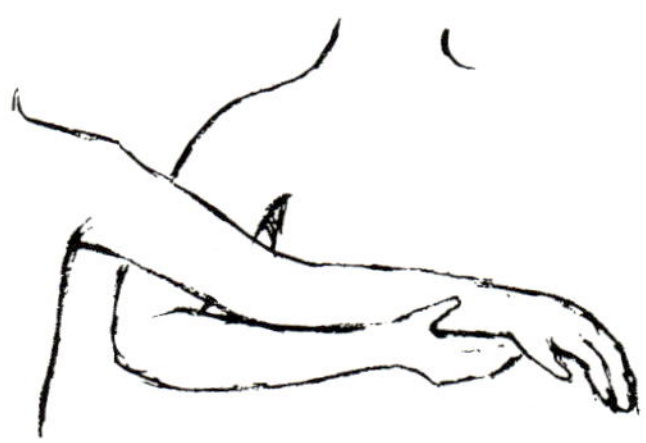

Fig. 27 *Short arm hold.*

3. The long arm hold provides a hand-on-hand situation. The arms of the child and those of the therapist are extended side-ways. To provide the child with a support that can be pushed against, the therapist's open hands are sloping upwards and inwards while the child's hands are placed on them sloping downwards and outwards (Fig. 28). This

Fig. 28 *The position of the hands in a long arm hold.*

hold is a progression on the short arm hold and is used when a greater degree of control is acquired by the child.

Holds for rolling in the horizontal

Rolling can be taught in several ways. When developing rolling on to the bar, the third hold described under 'Holds — backing' would be used (see p. 54).

1. Rolling arm-to-arm hold. The child is placed in supine lying at a right-angle to one side of the therapist, who supports the child at the level of the inferior angle of the scapulae with the arm on that side. To create a roll through 360° in front of the therapist, the child turns the head towards the therapist and brings the outer arm and leg across the body (Fig. 29). As the child's outer arm is brought across the body, the therapist's free arm supports and guides it as it moves, without contacting the child's thorax. When the rolling action is complete the child will again be at a right-angle to the therapist, supported as described above but on the side of the therapist opposite to that on which the rolling movement commenced.

Fig. 29 *The hold for rolling from arm to arm.*

2. As a progression towards developing independent rolling, the following hold is used. The therapist stands facing the child, the hands at the child's waist. A step is taken to one side and the child then lies back in a supine lying position. The therapist places the leg nearest to the child directly below the centre of balance of the child's body and bends the knee, keeping the foot flat on the floor of the pool. The outer leg is abducted and extended (Fig. 30). The therapist is now in a lunge position. The only further action the therapist makes as the child rolls is to pat the child's body round, the hands remaining at waist level. For safety, the roll must take place toward the therapist. In order to roll in the opposite direction, the therapist moves

Fig. 30 *Rolling hold — starting and finishing position.*

around the child's head to the other side. During this manoeuvre the therapist's hands maintain support at the centre of balance of the body.

The hold used for activities where the child requires some support but can turn round within the encircling arms is also used for those which develop lateral rotation in the vertical plane, such as 'Walking in space' (Fig. 31).

Modifications of holds

Modifications of holds are necessary with some

Fig. 31 *'Walking in space' hold.*

children, and such modifications are acceptable, but the ideal holds described and the principles of holding, particularly of holding at or close to the centre of balance of the body, should be borne in mind at all times.

The following are some of the more useful modifications.

1. Holding at the elbows when working in a circle with a group. In this instance the child may not be ready to transfer from a short arm to a long arm hold.

2. If a child has poor head control and is working with a group in a line or circle, creating a swinging action of the body forward and backward around the centre of buoyancy, it may be necessary to adapt a short arm hold. In this case the therapist's holding arm is externally rotated, bringing the child's arm into internal rotation, and the hand is held cupped ready to support the child's chin as the head comes forward. This can prevent sudden and frightening submersion of the face. If blowing is also not established as an automatic response, such action on the part of the therapist avoids difficulties which may arise from inhaling water. As soon as the child shows a degree of head control in prone, this modification should be withdrawn.

Holds for individual activities

The hold used for the activity 'Bells' when working individually with the child is as follows. The child is held in front of the therapist, supported around the waist with one arm, while the other hand is placed over the child's hands, which should be placed on the anterior aspect of the flexed legs just below the knees (Fig. 32).

It is essential that the child is held away from the therapist's body, otherwise appreciation of the swinging action of the body is not experienced and the need to use the head to control or create the swing not learnt. Where the child has difficulty in bringing the arms forward and maintaining this position, the therapist may need to assist the forward movement and hold the child's hands firmly on the knees. Alternatively, the therapist may place the child's hands under the knees between the thighs and calves, and hold the child's legs firmly

Fig. 32 *'Bells' hold.*

flexed, the hand being placed halfway between the knees and the ankles.

As the child gains control of vertical rotation, progression to a wider swing with extension of the body follows (as in the activity 'Rag dolls'), and a hold at the waist is used when working on an individual basis. The child is placed at the side of the therapist, the arm nearest to the child being placed across the back at waist level. The other arm is across the front of the therapist's body to the side of the child nearest to the therapist, again at waist level. As the therapist walks forwards, the child's body moves into the prone lying position. As the therapist walks backwards, the child flexes the entire body, extends the head and as the body rotates backwards it is extended to the supine lying position. When the child experiences difficulty in creating the movement from prone to supine, the therapist can facilitate the movement by using the forearms and elbow of the arm across the back in a downward and forward direction on the lumbar spine of the child.

Other holds for individual work with a child, some facing and backing, have already been described (see p. 52).

Disengagement

A major aim in water activity is total independence in the element if possible, and an important factor in the child's progress in learning the necessary skills is correct holding. However, if total independence is to be achieved, holds must be withdrawn gradually as the child becomes proficient in a skill and is able to perform it automatically and independently.

The art of knowing when and to what extent the hold can be withdrawn comes with experience. Constant observation and a feel for the child's ability within each activity act as a guide to disengagement. The most difficult point of disengagement is the final letting go. Frequently the child demands a hold, even if it is only by a fingertip. It appears to be a real hurdle to some children, despite mental adjustment and the ability to submerge at will.

Games

The significance and value of games and learning through play are well known and have been discussed by many authors (Freud, 1955; Erikson, 1963; Piaget, 1963). The word 'play' is applied to all the things children do for the joy of it, and it is suggested that for the child, play is a most important and serious activity (Stallibrass, 1977). A young child will begin to play spontaneously once the dependence on the early primitive reflexes disappears. The gradual integration of the child into the environment and the environment into the child is fostered by innate urges to develop relationships with other human beings and to acquire everyday skills through play (Sheridan, 1977). Sheridan also suggests that in play a child experiments with everything that is around, both people and things, and from this is able to develop concepts, language, intellect, emotional and social behaviours, and to control and adapt these to groups and society. Thus play provides a strong impetus towards growing up (Jolly, 1975) and is important to the optimal development of the child.

Disability frequently prevents the acquisition of skills because movement is impaired and development in some or all of its aspects is retarded, so the necessity for the provision of opportunities for play for disabled children needs to be recognised. Therapists can use play in treatment to achieve desired responses and there are the additional advantages of avoiding disinterest, boredom and antagonism towards treatment sessions (Reynell and Martin, 1965).

The author has found that in some instances the difference in a child's attitude to therapeutic activity on land and in water has been so marked that it has been advisable to cease physiotherapy on land temporarily and concentrate on activity in water. In this medium the children were happy, interested and responding. In due course it became possible to re-introduce land-based treatment sessions.

This approach applies to activity in water. Water tends to bring us all to the same level and provides an excellent means of widening the experience of the disabled child in many ways — physically, intellectually, socially and emotionally. Playing games helps to destroy the idea of 'treatment' and assists in the production of a greater response from the child. Where games are played in a group, the child is motivated by others in the group and provided with opportunities for socialisation.

Games should incorporate both therapeutic and recreational aspects. Many of these are similar and thus easily combined in an activity. The emphasis may be placed in one direction or the other throughout an activity or programme or may alternate between the two. If, for therapeutic reasons, emphasis needs to be placed on a joint or joints to increase range of motion and strengthen the muscles around the joints being exercised, an activity which provides the required movements would be chosen or the therapist would use ingenuity to develop such a game. Because each game has a particular aim or aims directed towards achieving recreational objectives and skills, games should never be selected randomly.

When developing games, the following points need to be considered:

(a) the objective or skill required,
(b) the appreciation by the child of the skill,
(c) position for the activity or transition from one position to another,
(d) the formation for a group and changes of formation,
(e) the movements involved,
(f) rotational control,
(g) control and/or movement of the limbs,
(h) head control,
(i) breathing control,
(j) the means of progression.

Development of the games should occur in such a manner that the skill being taught becomes gradually automatic and is performed correctly and independently. The method of development of games can be readily seen in the examples which follow in the text.

Other psychosocial factors requiring attention when constructing an activity are:

(a) degree of participation,
(b) the development of water confidence and mental adjustment,
(c) the provision of opportunities for the expression of personality and enjoyment,
(d) the use of songs, music and rhythm.

Explanations of the game should be short and explicit. Equipment may be used to encourage movement, to add to enjoyment, or to facilitate the acquisition of learning skils. When used it should be as simple as possible. The atmosphere and pace of an activity can be increased or decreased by the use of the therapist's voice, tone and manner, and in the choice of song, music or rhythm. The child's interest and knowledge can be developed and extended by story telling, drama and the use of environmental factors. The development of breathing control, control of the head, trunk and limbs, and the creation of appropriate movement of these body parts not only assists in the recreational skill of swimming, but considerably enhances body image, spatial relationships and an awareness of the body as a whole unit.

In view of the similarity of both therapeutic and recreational goals, it is not intended that the description give more than a brief indication of the purpose of each activity. The therapist will be aware that the encouragement of:

(a) relaxation,
(b) movement,
(c) head control,
(d) balance control,
(e) rotational control,
(f) the extremes of posture and increased range of movement,
(g) body image and spatial awareness,
(h) breathing control,

is present to a greater or lesser degree in each activity, and so can develop these in either a therapeutic or recreational direction as required.

Breathing control forms a basis for all activities and is as necessary for swimming as it is for helping respiratory control. The acquisition of lip closure, pursing the lips and blowing appears to improve the development of speech and feeding patterns.

Mental adjustment to the element of water involves aspects of perceptual and learning skills in addition to the acquisition of gross and fine motor skills.

The ability to restore the body's balance and maintain it against any disturbing forces has implications for head control, balance and coordination. In addition, rotational control assists the child therapeutically, as well as allowing for the achievement of swimming with all the implications that pertain to acquiring the art.

Many of the activities described in the following pages have been drawn from the Halliwick Method. Some of these activities have been included in books such as *Duffield's Exercise in Water* (Skinner and Thomson, 1983) and *Swimming for the Disabled* (Association of Swimming Therapy, 1981). All the games have been designed to teach the skills required of the swimmer and are closely interwoven with the ten-point programme of the method. Price (1980), discussing swimming for the physically handicapped child, cites the ten-point programme as developing the following.

1. Mental adjustment.
2. Disengagement.
3. Vertical rotation control.
4. Lateral rotation control.
5. Combined rotation.
6. Use of upthrust.
7. Balance is stillness.
8. Turbulent gliding.
9. A simple progression.
10. A basic movement.

The programme also describes the tasks involved in each stage. Since, in the Halliwick Method, each game has a teaching point related to the above stages, an orderly progression takes place from total dependence to the total independence of the person in the water.

For clarity, the games and activities in this text have been divided into sections related to their main purpose. In some instances more than one skill is required and such games will be listed under each heading.

The sections for activities are as follows.

1. Mental adjustment and disengagement.
2. Development of rotational control.
3. Development of balance and co-ordination.
4. Dynamic activity.

Although the activities have been categorised in this manner, it does not mean that the child must be able to carry out all the skills in one section before passing on to the next. For instance, mental adjustment and disengagement occur on a continuum throughout the activities though the need for mental adjustment lessens as skills are acquired. It may be necessary to support the child as each new skill is tackled, but disengagement is more rapidly achieved as the child progresses. Similarly, activities that develop rotational control will overlap with those for balance and co-ordination, and all lead into dynamic independent activity.

ACTIVITIES FOR MENTAL ADJUSTMENT AND DISENGAGEMENT

The activities under this heading are particularly suitable for mental adjustment and disengagement (Table 4; pp. 66–96). They provide the means by which the child can progress from the initial stages of dependence on the therapist to becoming adjusted to the element of water and able to work either alone or with minimal support. Both mental adjustment and disengagement continue throughout the activities for rotational control, balance and co-ordination. The degree of mental adjustment required will diminish with the child's decreasing need for support as well as with the increased understanding of the element of water and ability in the medium.

When a new skill is introduced it may be necessary for the therapist to provide some support again. However, the length of time that this support will be required will be reduced and disengagement takes place more rapidly than hitherto.

Entry into the water has already been described (see p. 42). It plays a large part in the mental adjustment of the child and must be handled appropriately. Suitable songs and rhymes for entry are provided in the text (see p. 50). Once the child is in the water there should be no hesitation. It is important that an activity follows immediately upon entry. For instance, having used 'Humpty Dumpty' as a means of entry, encouraging the child to come forward towards the water, entering on the therapist's words 'had a great fall', the next two lines should proceed smoothly into jumping and blowing activities as the therapist and child move away from the side of the pool. In this way the child's attention is distracted and any anxieties about being in water allayed.

Table 4 Activities for mental adjustment and disengagement

1. Jumping
2. Here we go round the mulberry bush
3. Stepping stones; Giant strides; Fairy strides
4. Clocks and watches
5. Ring a ring of roses
6. There was a crooked man
7. How wide, how tall
8. Hickory, Dickory Dock
9. We reach up tall together
10. Come with me
11. Blowing objects along the surface of the water
12. I'm forever blowing bubbles
13. Walking around and across the circle
14. If you're happy and you know it
15. Puffer train (or Hedi, hedi, ho)

JUMPING

A 'stick' and 'ball' activity suitable for a group and also the individual. Jumping in this form should be used immediately following entry.

Jumping as an activity leads towards independence in water and can be adapted and used in various activities as part of a pattern of movement. Whether jumping forwards or backwards, the head should be kept forward. In the early stages of water activity it is more appropriate for the swimmer to jump forwards and the supporting therapist to move backwards. Later, jumping backwards and even sideways can be introduced to the swimmer. Many rhymes and songs about jumping are available for use in this activity and encourage rhythmic movement and breathing control.

Therapeutic aims

1. To develop head control in the anterior/posterior direction.
2. To encourage movement of the body, especially flexion and extension of the body as a whole.
3. To encourage control of the upper limbs.
4. To improve balance and co-ordination.
5. To improve respiration and breathing control.

Jumping

	Primary activity	*Intermediate activity*	*Advanced activity*
Purpose	Mental adjustment and vertical rotational control	As primary	As primary
Appreciation	The need for forward action of the head to maintain vertical balance	As primary	As primary
Formation	The swimmer is facing the therapist with hands on the therapist's shoulders and supported at the waist	As primary, but a hands on hands hold is used (see p. 53)	As primary, except that no support is given to the swimmer
Instruction	'Jump and blow.' The swimmer is encouraged to bend the knees up to the chest when jumping and to extend the legs for landing, but to keep the head forward and blow onto the surface of the water	'Jump and blow — blow into the water.' The swimmer uses the upturned hands of the therapist as a base from which to work. The hands must remain below the surface, otherwise the swimmer's balance will be disturbed	'Jump and blow — keep your head and your hands forward.' The therapist walks backwards in front of the swimmer who is reaching forward with the hands towards the therapist. At first the swimmer may only blow onto the water, but at the intermediate level the swimmer must be able to blow into the water and at the advanced level should be able to submerge, blowing strongly, and maintain balance totally independently

'HERE WE GO ROUND THE MULBERRY BUSH'

A 'stick' activity played in a circle and suitable for a group of young children.

Therapeutic aims

1. To develop head control in all directions.
2. To improve and maintain the range of movement in the cervical spine.
3. To improve balance and co-ordination.
4. To develop body image and awareness.
5. To improve respiration and breathing control.
6. To increase the range of movement in the hip joints and of trunk-side flexion.
7. To develop awareness of skills of daily living.

'Here we go round the mulberry bush'

	Primary activity	*Intermediate activity*	*Advanced activity*
Purpose	Mental adjustment	As primary	As primary
Appreciation	The weight of water and how to enjoy water activity	As primary	As primary
Formation	A circle is formed of swimmers and therapists placed alternately using a short arm hold	As primary, except a long arm hold is used	As intermediate, but less support is given, the speed of activity increased, and changes in direction of the circle may be introduced at any time
Instruction (same for all three activities)	'We are all going to walk sideways like a crab and lean our heads and shoulders in the same direction. Push with your head and shoulders.' While singing 'Here we go round the mulberry bush', the circle moves sideways leaning against the water. A progression at this stage may involve the swimmer blowing into the water each time the word 'bush' is sung. Other skills involving mental adjustment and head control may be introduced as follows. 1. 'This is the way we blow bubbles' — the swimmer bringing the head forward and blowing. 2. 'This is the way we wash our ears' — the swimmer side flexes the head, first to one side and then the other, taking the ears close to the water. 3. 'This is the way we wash our hair' — the swimmer extends the head and cervical spine to place the occipital region in the water and turns the head from side to side. 4. 'This is the way we nod our heads' — the swimmer takes the head forwards and backwards slowly and rhythmically. The therapist can introduce any variations the imagination and ingenuity suggest.		

STEPPING STONES

A 'stick' activity.

Therapeutic aims

1. To develop rhythmical movement towards independence.
2. To encourage balance, co-ordination and postural reactions.
3. To increase and maintain range of movement.
4. To improve gait.
5. To increase mental adaptability.
6. To improve respiration and breathing control.

Stepping stones

	Primary activity	*Intermediate activity*	*Advanced activity*
Purpose	Mental adjustment and disengagement	As primary	As primary
Appreciation	The effect of forward action of the head on vertical balance control	As primary	As primary
Formation	The swimmer faces the therapist with the hands on the therapist's shoulders. The therapist supports the swimmer at the waist	A hands on hands hold is used	The therapist is behind the swimmer supporting at the waist or not, depending on the swimmer's ability. Alternatively, the therapist may remain in front, no support being provided
Instruction	'We are going to step from one stone to another across the pool.' The swimmer is encouraged to take larger and larger steps	As primary	The swimmer is encouraged to jump from one leg to the other

GIANT STRIDES

A 'stick' activity suitable for individual work. A group of swimmers and therapists working in pairs could use this activity.

Therapeutic aims

1. To improve mental adaptability.
2. To encourage independent movement.
3. To encourage balance and co-ordination.
4. To improve head control.

FAIRY STRIDES

Fairy strides

This activity is played in the same manner as 'Giant strides'. The purpose, appreciation and formation are the same as in 'Giant strides', but the instruction to the swimmer is to take as small steps as possible.

A greater degree of balance control may be required when working on a small base.

Giant strides

	Primary activity	*Intermediate activity*	*Advanced activity*
Purpose	Mental adjustment and disengagement	As primary	As primary
Appreciation	The effect of movement through the water on the body	As primary	As primary
Formation	The swimmer faces the therapist, who uses a facing waist hold (see p. 52). If the swimmer's ability permits, a hands on hands hold may be employed (see p. 53)	The therapist stands behind the swimmer using the backing waist hold (see p. 54)	As intermediate, but no support is given to the swimmer
Instruction	'We are going to walk like giants, with big steps across the pool.' The therapist walks backwards encouraging the swimmer to take as large a step as possible	As primary. The swimmer may need to be reminded to keep the hands forward just under the surface of the water	'Walk with giant strides across the pool'

CLOCKS AND WATCHES, OR 'THE GRAND-FATHER'S CLOCK'

A 'stick' activity for groups or individuals.

Therapeutic aims

1. To improve and maintain head control laterally.
2. To encourage and develop balance and co-ordination.
3. To develop spatial awareness.
4. To improve respiration and breathing control.
5. To increase mental adaptability.
6. To heighten awareness of the ability to lean against water and use it as a force with which to work.

Clocks and watches, or 'The Grandfather's clock'

	Primary activity	*Intermediate activity*	*Advanced activity*
Purpose	Head control in a lateral direction; appreciation of the weight out of water	As primary	As primary
Appreciation	Water has weight and can be leant against	As primary	As primary
Formation	The swimmer faces the therapist placing the hands on the therapist's shoulders, support being given to the swimmer at the waist	A hands on hands hold is used	The swimmer is not supported and in the case of a child using the therapist's thighs as a base, a finger-tip hold is given
Instruction	'Let's tick from side to side slowly like a grandfather clock.' The swimmer moves the head to one side to initiate the ticking action and then leans and steps to the opposite side. These actions are repeated with an increasing range of movements of the head and abduction of the legs. When the swimmer is too small to have the feet on the floor of the pool, the therapist's thighs provide a base (see p. 12)	As primary, and this can be varied to include ticking faster like a watch	As intermediate

'RING A RING O' ROSES'

A 'stick' activity suitable for a group.

Therapeutic aims

1. To improve head control laterally.
2. To improve abduction/adduction of the hips (if the child is able to reach the floor of the pool with the feet), and trunk side flexion.
3. To improve and maintain balance and co-ordination.
4. To improve respiration and breathing control.
5. To increase mental adaptability.

A number of verses to this nursery rhyme may be found in *This Little Puffin — Nursery Songs and Rhymes* (Matterson, 1969).

Many songs and nursery rhymes may be used in a similar manner to 'Ring o' roses'. All are 'stick' activities and develop the same skills. Variation in direction can be introduced as suggested, and dis-engagement and lateral rotation in the vertical developed if the swimmers are asked to disengage and turn to face out of the circle and back again. They must observe the direction in which the circle is moving, leaning the head and shoulders correctly whether facing out of or into the circle.

Examples of songs and rhymes are:

'Dr Foster went to Gloucester'
'There was a crooked man'
'Here we go round the mulberry bush'
'Baa, baa, black sheep'
'Waltzing Matilda'

The creative therapist will find it possible to introduce variation into the the activities described — particularly for older children, teenagers or adults — by the choice of contemporary songs. Many variations can be introduced in these activities and a few of these are described in the following text.

'Ring a ring o' roses'

	Primary activity	*Intermediate activity*	*Advanced activity*
Purpose	Head control; water has weight	As primary	As primary
Appreciation	The weight of water and the fact that it can be leaned against	As primary	As primary
Formation	A circle is formed with alternate swimmer and therapist, using a short arm hold	As primary, but a long arm hold is used	As intermediate
Instruction	'We are going to walk sideways like a crab taking a step and bringing the feet together.' 'Ring a ring o' roses a pocket full of posies A-tishoo, A-tishoo We all go blow' At this stage it is inadvisable to use the phrase 'We all fall down'. The circle moves round, leaning with the head and shoulders in the direction of movement. Blowing is encouraged on to the surface of the water	As primary. Changes of direction can be introduced. The swimmers must develop head control and lean in the new direction without losing the rhythm and must continue to blow into the water	As intermediate, and the swimmer is encouraged to submerge, blowing. At this stage the words 'We all fall down' may be introduced

'THERE WAS A CROOKED MAN'

A 'stick' activity suitable for a group.

Therapeutic aims

1. To improve head control.
2. To improve balance and co-ordination.
3. To increase range of abduction/adduction of the hips.
4. To increase mental adaptability.
5. To improve respiration and breathing control.

'There was a crooked man'

	Primary activity	*Intermediate activity*	*Advanced activity*
Purpose	Head control laterally	As primary	As primary
Appreciation	Water has weight	As primary	As primary
Formation	A circle is formed of alternate swimmer and therapist using a long arm hold	As primary	As primary
Instruction	'Walk round sideways like a crab.' To the words of 'There was a crooked man', in a very definite rhythm, the circle moves in one direction	Walk round sideways 'like a crab' and when the group leader says 'change', the circle changes direction. Therapists must ensure that when 'change' is called, the swimmers push their heads in the opposite direction *without* losing their rhythm and that 'blowing' is automatic	Walk round sideways 'like a crab' changing direction at the instruction 'change' and jumping into the centre when saying the last line — 'And they all lived together in a little wooden house'. By introducing changes of direction both sideways and forwards, the swimmer is given more to do and think about while at the same time maintaining the rhythm. The therapist watches for automatic reactions of head control and 'blowing'

HOW WIDE? HOW TALL?

A 'stick' activity suitable for group or individual work.

Therapeutic aims

1. To develop body image and spatial awareness.
2. To improve balance and co-ordination.
3. To increase mental adaptability.
4. To increase and maintain range of movement in the shoulder and hip joints.

How wide? How tall?

	Primary activity	*Intermediate activity*	*Advanced activity*
Purpose	Body image; spatial awareness and disengagement	As primary	As primary
Appreciation	How large the body is	As primary	As primary
Formation	The child faces the therapist who stabilises the upright position of the child at waist level	As primary	As primary, but no stabilisation is given
Instruction	'Spread your arms sideways and see how wide you are.' 'How tall are you?' 'Stretch your arms above your head.' 'Cuddle me.'	As primary, but the child is encouraged to spread the legs as well as the arms apart, and to stand on tiptoe when reaching up	As intermediate. The instruction 'Cuddle me' can be altered to 'Put your hands on my shoulders' if desirable for any reason — for example, a child demonstrating a distaste for such an action or in the case of the adult

'HICKORY, DICKORY, DOCK'

A 'stick' activity suitable for group or individual work for young children.

Therapeutic aims

1. To improve head control.
2. To encourage balance and co-ordination.
3. To develop independent movement.
4. To increase mental adaptability.
5. To increase range of movement in the upper limbs and abduction of the hip.
6. To improve respiration and breathing control.

'Hickory, dickory, dock'

	Primary activity	*Intermediate activity*	*Advanced activity*
Purpose	Encourage disengagement, balance and head control	As primary	As primary
Appreciation	The need for head-forward position to maintain balance	As primary	As primary
Formation (same for all three activites)	The swimmer stands facing the therapist. In the case of small children out of their depth, they may stand on the therapist's bent knees. The therapist holds the swimmer at the centre of bouyancy, i.e. about waist level, hands on hips		
Instruction	'We sing "Hickory, dickory, dock" ', ticking like a clock from side to side. Climb the clock by climbing up your therapist as 'The mouse runs up the clock'; clap hands over your head when 'The clock strikes'; 'run' down your therapist and 'blow' as 'The mouse runs down', repeating the 'ticking'. In the primary activity the therapist will be giving maximum assistance	As primary. Now the swimmer must climb up and down with less assistance. When 'ticking', stabilisation at waist level only should be required. There is a danger of falling forwards or backwards when in a triangular shape, which gives some lateral stability but none antero-posteriorly	As primary. To ensure lateral stability, the therapist can push the swimmer gently, but firmly, from side to side in the 'ticking' and see if the swimmer restores to the triangular position and is controlling body forwards and backwards. All climbing should be done independently and, when standing on the therapist's knees high out of water, the swimmer should control the body's balance without assistance if possible. If not, minimum help is given by the therapist. Blowing must be automatic when 'The mouse runs down'

WE REACH UP TALL TOGETHER

A 'ball' and 'stick' activity.

Therapeutic aims

1. To encourage and maintain movement of the head, trunk and all four limbs.
2. To improve body image and spatial awareness.
3. To improve balance and co-ordination.
4. To improve respiration and breathing control.
5. To improve mental adaptability.

We reach up tall together

	Primary activity	*Intermediate activity*	*Advanced activity*
Purpose	Extremes of posture; disengagement; vertical rotation; head control; control of movement; balance and upthrust	As primary	As primary
Appreciation	The use of the head to control the body; body image	As primary	As primary
Formation	The therapist supports the swimmer at the waist from behind	The swimmer is given less support throughout and in the second verse faces the therapist using a hands on hands hold	The swimmer is given the minimum of assistance or no assistance

Instruction (same for all three activities)

'Reach up tall.' The swimmer stretches the arms above the head while singing or saying:

'We reach up tall together
We reach up tall together
We reach up tall together
Like giraffes at the zoo'.

'Curl up small.' The swimmer curls the body up as small as possible while singing or saying:

'We curl up small together
We curl up small together
We curl up small together
Like pussy likes to do'.

'Lie still in the water.' The swimmer 'sits', extends the head and allows the body to float in the supine lying position, supported at the waist by the therapist and with the head on the therapist's shoulder, and sings or says:

'We lie still in the water
We lie still in the water
We lie still in the water
Like all good children do'.

'Kick your legs.' The swimmer proceeds to kick the legs alternately in the supine lying position, singing or saying:

'We kick our legs together
We make it rainy weather
We kick our legs together
Until the skies turn blue'.

'Stand up.' The swimmer regains the upright position by flexing the knees to the chest, brings the head and arms forward until the body is rotated to the vertical and then remains standing, balanced, while singing or saying:

'We stand up in the sunshine
We stand up in the sunshine
We stand up in the sunshine
And blow our bubbles too',

On the last line the swimmer demonstrates blowing

COME WITH ME

A 'stick' activity suitable for group and individual work. 'Swimming', 'paddling', 'floating', 'kicking' and 'rolling' are other actions that could be employed as the swimmer becomes more competent.

In the primary activity the swimmer would be supported in the supine lying position. In the intermediate activity, less support would be given. At the advanced level, the swimmer would be able to move independently through the water. Attaining the supine lying position and recovering introduce the extremes of posture and vertical rotational control.

Therapeutic aims

1. To encourage and develop movement and the control of movement.
2. To improve balance and co-ordination.
3. To develop body and spatial awareness and other perceptual skills.
4. To improve respiration and breathing control.
5. To increase mental adaptability.

Come with me

	Primary activity	*Intermediate activity*	*Advanced activity*
Purpose	Mental adjustment, movement and control of movement, balance and rotational control	As primary	As primary
Appreciation	The head controls the feet; awareness of movement through water effects	As primary	As primary
Formation	The swimmer faces the therapist with hands on the therapist's shoulders. Support is given at the swimmer's waist. A line formation or free order is used	The swimmer and therapist are facing using a hands on hands hold	The swimmer works independently. The therapist is nearby, at first in front and later behind the swimmer. Finally the swimmer is able to achieve the actions alone
Instruction	'Come walking with me, Come walking with me, Over the highway and down to the sea, come walking with me.' Variations such as jumping, hopping, tiptoe and dancing may be used	As primary. A further progression may be introduced in which the therapist supports the swimmer at the waist from behind	As intermediate, with minimal or no support

BLOWING OBJECTS ALONG THE SURFACE OF THE WATER (Fig. 33)

A 'stick' activity suitable for group and individual work.

Whether facing or backing holds are used, the child should be kept in front of the therapist as vertical rotational control is also developed in this activity.

Fig. 33 *Blowing an object across the water.*

Therapeutic aims

1. To develop head control.
2. To develop and maintain breathing control.
3. To increase balance and co-ordination.
4. To improve mental adaptability.

Blowing objects along the surface of the water

	Primary activity	*Intermediate activity*	*Advanced activity*
Purpose	Head and breathing control	As primary	As primary
Appreciation	The effect of blowing on the head and body	As primary	As primary
Formation	The swimmer faces the therapist and places the hands on the therapist's shoulders. The therapist supports the child at the waist. A bath toy is placed between the faces on the surface of the water	The swimmer faces away from the therapist, who supports the child at the waist	As intermediate
Instruction	'Blow the duck (fish, table tennis ball, "poached egg", etc.) to me and I will blow it back to you.' The therapist should remain stationary at first as any movement backwards will cause the object to move away from the child's face due to turbulent effect. However, as a progression, such action can take place and the author has found that towing the object away in this manner may focus the child's attention, and bring the head, eyes and often the hands (if they are not on the therapist's shoulders) to midline	'Put the duck on the water in front of you; keep your arms forward and blow the duck across the pool.'	As intermediate. An incentive, such as a race, will increase the speed and depth of the blowing action. The aim is to encourage the blowing to proceed from blowing regularly on to the surface to blowing regularly into the water

'I'M FOREVER BLOWING BUBBLES'

A 'stick' activity suitable for a group. As an individual activity, walking sideways across the pool may be used.

It is possible to alter the words to make the activity more appropriate for water — for example, exchange the word 'sea' for 'air'. Other lines can be made to rhyme by the use of words such as 'whirl' and 'swirl'.

Therapeutic aims

1. To encourage and maintain head control in the vertical.
2. To improve balance and co-ordination.
3. To encourage the movements required in walking sideways and forwards.
4. To improve and maintain respiration and breathing control.

'I'm forever blowing bubbles'

	Primary activity	*Intermediate activity*	*Advanced activity*
Purpose	Head control	As primary	As primary
Appreciation	Effect of head movement on body; water has weight	As primary	As primary
Formation	A circle with alternate swimmer and therapist using a short arm hold	As primary, but a long arm hold is used	As intermediate with swimmers inside the circle
Instruction	'Walk sideways and whenever the word "blowing" is said, blow into the water.'	As primary	'Walk anywhere in the circle or across it singing and blowing.'

WALKING AROUND AND ACROSS THE CIRCLE

A 'stick' activity suitable for a group.

Therapeutic aims

1. To improve head control.
2. To encourage active movement and increase the range of movement.
3. To improve mental adaptability.
4. To increase respiration and breathing control.
5. To improve balance and co-ordination and spatial awareness.

	Primary activity	*Intermediate activity*	*Advanced activity*
Purpose	Mental adjustment and disengagement	As primary	As primary
Appreciation	Increasing ability to move in water independently	As primary	As primary
Formation	The swimmer faces the therapist and places the hands on the therapist's shoulders. A circle is formed by all the therapists joining hands	As primary	As primary

Walking around and across the circle

Instruction

'While we stand still, walk your hands along our arms all the way round the circle to the right (or left).' The swimmers must all go in the same direction, and are verbally encouraged to move round the circle passing each therapist in turn.

If a swimmer's feet do not touch the floor of the pool, dependence on the arms and hands is greater and head control to maintain the vertical position must be well developed. Crossing the hands and arms while moving around the circle is inadvisable, especially when the child's condition produces strong flexion, adduction and medial rotation of the shoulders with extension at the elbows. However, in circumstances where crossing the body's midline is to be encouraged, such an action can prove helpful

'Walk round the circle close to us but do not hold on.'

Alternatively, the swimmers could hold the therapists' arms and move around the circle while the circle itself moves in one direction and then another. This would require greater control from the swimmers, especially against the turbulence created by the therapists' movements

'Walk around and across the circle without holding on.' Some swimmers may choose to jump across, others will attempt to swim. For the child who cannot touch the bottom of the pool, swimming across is encouraged. In this case a therapist may choose to come into the centre of the circle to assist any swimmers who may be uncertain of their ability. A further progression could be made by having the swimmers walk round the outside of the circle

'IF YOU ARE HAPPY AND YOU KNOW IT'

A combined 'ball' and 'stick' activity suitable for individual and group work. Any therapeutic activity can be introduced into the words of the song.

Therapeutic aims

1. To encourage head control.
2. To improve balance and co-ordination.
3. To improve and maintain respiration and breathing control.
4. To improve body image and spatial awareness.
5. To develop control of the limbs and encourage awareness of the head for control.
6. To encourage active movement of the trunk and limbs.
7. To improve mental adaptability.

'If you are happy and you know it'

	Primary activity	*Intermediate activity*	*Advanced activity*
Purpose	Head control; disengagement; control of the limbs and balance	As primary	As primary
Appreciation	The effect of movement of the head, arms and legs on the balance of the body	As primary	As primary
Formation	This may vary from a circle with alternate swimmer and therapist to the swimmer either facing the therapist or facing away	This may be altered to encourage disengagement. A circle may change to the swimmer facing the therapist	The swimmer works independently, little or no support being provided
Instruction	To perform the action required by following the therapist's instructions. For example, 'If you're happy and you know it, bend your knees' or 'blow some bubbles' or 'make some waves'. The therapist will give the appropriate support to allow the swimmer to achieve the required action	As primary	As primary. More advanced skills, such as submerging when blowing bubbles or mushroom floats (see p. 154) or rolling, can be introduced

'PUFFER TRAIN' OR 'HEDI, HEDI, HO' (Fig. 34)

A 'stick' activity suitable for group work.

This activity should be taken slowly and gently at first, especially with young children, with whom it is a great favourite. As an alternative to the train, 'Hedi, hedi, ho' can be sung and the elephant's trunk tries to catch the tail.

Therapeutic aims

1. To improve mental adaptability.
2. To increase head control.
3. To encourage balance and co-ordination.
4. To improve and maintain respiration and breathing control.

Fig. 34 *Line formation for 'Puffer train'.*

'Puffer train' (or 'Hedi, hedi, ho')

	Primary activity	*Intermediate activity*	*Advanced activity*
Purpose	Mental adjustment; head control and balance	As primary	As primary
Appreciation	Water has weight and can be leaned against; turbulent effect	As primary	As primary
Formation	Alternate swimmer and therapist in a line behind each other. The first therapist in the line may circle the swimmer with the arms or use a forearm bicycle hold. The next and all other therapists take the arms forward *under* the swimmer's arms and grasp the therapist in front *around* the waist. The line is closely linked in this way and each child is secure and feels safe. Where a swimmer has strongly extended arms or marked lack of control of these limbs, the therapist may hold the wrists and take the swimmer's arms forward and around the waist of the therapist in front, maintaining them in this position.	As primary, except that the hold is changed to each swimmer holding around the waist of the therapist in front and each therapist holds around the swimmer's waist	As primary, but the swimmer is placed behind the therapist

Instruction	As we sing 'Puffer train', the line will move around the pool in any direction the leader chooses. At the end of the verse the 'driver of the train' tries to catch the 'guard' at the end. The therapists at the end of the line must encourage the swimmers to lean away from the direction in which the 'driver' is approaching. Once the 'guard' has been caught, a new swimmer takes the lead and the activity is repeated. Each swimmer is the responsibility of a therapist and it is essential that the swimmer is observed to ensure that breathing control is encouraged and that the swimmer does lean from side to side appropriately	As primary. It is important that the therapist watches the swimmer's hold and encourages the appropriate actions at all times	As primary. The turbulence in this activity is considerable and the swimmer may be dragged off by it. The therapist must be aware of this possibility and watch carefully to cope with this contingency should it arise. Initially the swimmer's hands may be held by one of the therapist's, therefore the other arm and hand of the therapist connect with the swimmer in front

ACTIVITIES FOR THE DEVELOPMENT OF ROTATIONAL CONTROL

Activities for the development of rotational control can be divided into the following.

1. Vertical rotational control.
2. Lateral rotational control in the vertical and horizontal planes.
3. Combined rotational control.
4. Control of buoyancy or upthrust effects.

Notes related to each of these divisions precede the descriptions of the activities (see also Table 5).

VERTICAL ROTATION

The activities contained in this section are designed to help the child create and control all movements around the centre of buoyancy of the body in a forward and backward direction. The child is able to maintain the upright position and move from it either to supine lying or prone lying and recover to the vertical or upright posture.

Table 5a Activities for the development of rotational control

Vertical rotation

1. Bells
2. Little boy blue
3. Catch an object (ducks, fish in the pond, catching toes, reach for the bar, eggs for breakfast)
4. Rag dolls or swinging backwards and forwards
5. Wind, sun and rain
6. Bicycles
7. Charlie is over the water
8. The grand old Duke of York
9. Here we go Looby Loo
10. The wheels of the bus
11. Red red robin
12. Over the arches; Under the arches
13. Walking in space (see also Lateral rotation — vertical plane)
14. Little boats are on the sea

Bells

A 'ball' activity suitable for group and individual work.

At this level of activity a further progression could be that of encouraging the swimmer to extend the body in the supine and prone lying position, curling up to create the swing from one position to the other. Good head control is required at this stage to ensure that no sudden upswing of the legs occurs.

When using this activity on an individual basis, the therapist uses the hold described on p. 59. As the swimmer progresses to the advanced level the therapist can support at the waist. This support can be removed gradually until the swimmer is performing the activity independently.

Therapeutic aims

1. To develop head control.
2. To encourage active flexion and extension of the whole body.
3. To develop awareness of the extremes of posture and body image.
4. To improve co-ordination.
5. To increase mental adaptability.
6. To improve respiration and breathing control.

Bells

	Primary activity	*Intermediate activity*	*Advanced activity*
Purpose	Vertical rotational control	As primary	As primary
Appreciation	The effect of the movement of the head on the body position in the water	As primary	As primary
Formation	A circle is formed of alternate swimmers and therapists using a short arm hold	As primary	As primary except that a long arm hold is used
Instruction	'Swimmers, bend your knees to your chests, heads back slowly, heads forward and blow.' When necessary, facilitation and/or control of the body swing can be provided by the therapist through the supporting arms	'Let's sing "Ding dong bell" as we swing forwards and backwards.' A slow rhythm is important and the therapist watches for head control and breathing control while giving less assistance to the body swing	As intermediate

'LITTLE BOY BLUE'

A 'ball' and 'stick' activity suitable for group or individual work.

Therapeutic aims

1. To improve head control.
2. To improve and maintain balance and co-ordination.
3. To encourage body and spatial awareness.
4. To increase mental adaptability.
5. To improve respiration.
6. To encourage flexion/extension patterns of the whole body.
7. To increase the range of abduction/adduction in the hip joints.

'Little boy blue'

	Primary activity	*Intermediate activity*	*Advanced activity*
Purpose	Vertical rotation, head control	As primary	As primary
Appreciation	Effect of head movement on the body	As primary	As primary
Formation	A circle is formed of alternate swimmer and therapist using a short arm hold	As primary	As primary but using a long arm hold
Instruction	'Blow when the word "blow" is sung. Put the ear to the water to "hear the horn". Keep still when singing "fast asleep".'	As primary except lie back, remain still and go 'fast asleep'	As intermediate but the circle moves round, first in one direction and then the other, progressing further by frequent change of direction

CATCH AN OBJECT

Included under this title are activities such as 'Eggs for breakfast', 'Reach for the bar' and 'Catching toes'.

Therapeutic aims

1. To develop flexion/extension patterns of the whole body.
2. To encourage and maintain balance and co-ordination.
3. To improve rotational control in the anterior/posterior direction.
4. To improve control of the arms, reach and grasp symmetrically and asymmetrically if required.
5. To develop body image, spatial awareness and laterality (if
6. To improve respiration and breathing control.

	Primary activity	*Intermediate activity*	*Advanced activity*
Purpose	Vertical rotational control	As primary	As primary
Appreciation	The effect of head movement on the body	As primary	As primary
Formation	The swimmer in front of and facing away from the therapist. The backing hold (Fig. 23, p. 54) is used.	As primary but less support and assistance are given	As intermediate but support is only given to the floating position. The circle may be widened further and a competitive note introduced if one object is removed each time the activity is played

Catch an object

Instruction

' "Sit" in your chair hands forward, head back slowly until you are lying in bed, your head on my shoulder and go to sleep. When the bell sounds, you bend your knees up to your chest, bring your head and hands forwards, blow and get a "fish".' Ducks, eggs, rings, the bar or other swimmers' toes may be used as the objects to catch. If reaching for the bar, the swimmer and therapist should be facing the side of the pool and when the swimmer lies back, the toes should rest just touching the wall. At no time should a swimmer be permitted to catch the toes behind the bar as this may prove dangerous as the recovery action is made. The bell rings and the swimmers create a forward recovery and take an object. This activity is known at 'Eggs for breakfast' in the Halliwick Method but can also be developed as 'Ducks for dinner', 'Fish for lunch', 'Reach for the bar', 'Catching toes' and so on

As primary. The circle can be widened so that the swimmer has to reach forward a greater distance on recovering

The therapist must ensure that the swimmer controls the movement from the vertical to lying position with the head. This action should occur slowly as flotation is required. The correct starting position with the arms forward can be developed if the swimmer places the object in the centre of the circle and holds the object there until ready to lie back. When recovering forward, the swimmer will only be interested in reaching for an object whereas the therapist's concern is with ensuring the the correct movement pattern is created together with breathing control

BICYCLES

A 'ball' activity that can be used individually or in a group.

Variations of this activity can be introduced and a range of songs used. Bicycling is enjoyed by the children and may form part of an activity as, for example, in 'Here we go Looby Loo' or 'The wheels of the bus'. Alternatively, it may be used as an activity on its own and progressed to a competitive level.

The therapist must ensure that the child is not lifted out of the water and that head control and breathing control are developed. Therapeutically, strong flexion of the body is achieved in addition to head control, balance and flexion/extension movements of the lower limbs.

Therapeutic aims

1. To improve and maintain head control in anterior/posterior direction.
2. To encourage active movements of flexion/ extension in the lower limbs.
3. To encourage control of the upper limbs symmetrically.
4. To improve respiration and breathing control.
5. To develop and maintain balance and co-ordination.
6. To develop flexion of the body as a whole.
7. To improve mental adaptability.

	Primary activity	Intermediate activity	Advanced activity
Purpose	Vertical rotational control	As primary	As primary
Appreciation	The head controls the feet	As primary	As primary
Formation	The swimmer in front of the therapist, facing away. A bicycle forearm hold is used (p. 55)	As primary but the bicycle fist hold is used (p. 55)	As primary but a bicycle thumb hold is used (p. 55)
Instruction	'Bend your knees up to your chest and make your legs go round and round like riding a bicycle.' The swimmer uses the head to maintain the curled-up body in the vertical position while alternately flexing and extending the legs as if riding a bicycle. Verbal facilitation in regard to head control may be given. If the swimmer's legs come up towards the surface in front, then the instruction is directed towards a forward head movement. Should the swimmer's body go too far forwards, the instruction is to extend the head until the body is vertical again. Manual facilitation may be given by the therapist to the swimmer's forearm. The hold is not altered or lost	As primary but the activity is played more energetically	As primary but it is played extremely energetically and may take the form of a race across the pool

'CHARLIE IS OVER THE WATER'

A 'ball' activity suitable for a group. This is a variation on 'Bicycles' and is played to the rhyme:

'Charlie is over the water
Charlie is over the sea
Charlie caught a blackbird
But he can't catch me.'

Therapeutic aims

1. To improve and maintain head control in an anterior/posterior direction.
2. To encourage control of the upper limbs.
3. To develop active flexion and extension of the lower limbs.
4. To improve respiration and breathing control.
5. To encourage flexion of the body as a whole.
6. To increase mental adaptability.

'Charlie is over the water'

	Primary activity	*Intermediate activity*	*Advanced activity*
Purpose	Vertical rotational control	As primary	As primary
Appreciation	The effect of the head movement on the body	As primary	As primary
Formation	One therapist and swimmer act as 'Charlie', using a bicycle forearm hold. The remaining therapists and swimmers, using the same hold, form a circle around 'Charlie'	As primary, but the hold is changed to the second bicycle hold (see Fig. 25b, p. 56)	As primary, except the bicycle hold using the thumbs is used (see Fig. 25c, p. 56)
Instruction	As the group repeats the rhyme, the circle bicycles around in one direction, and on the last time 'Charlie' bicycles after the other swimmers, endeavouring to catch someone. The swimmer who is caught then becomes 'Charlie', and the activity is repeated	As primary, but the game is played more vigorously	As primary. The speed of the game is increased further

'THE GRAND OLD DUKE OF YORK'

A 'ball' activity suitable for group or individual work.

Therapeutic aims

1. To improve and maintain head control in an anterior/posterior direction.
2. To encourage control of the upper limbs.
3. To develop active flexion/extension of the lower limbs, and flexion of the body as a whole.
4. To improve respiration and breathing control.
5. To improve spatial awareness.
6. To encourage mental adaptability.

'The grand old Duke of York'

	Primary activity	*Intermediate activity*	*Advanced activity*
Purpose	Vertical rotational control	As primary	As primary
Appreciation	The effect of the head in controlling the body position	As primary	As primary
Formation	The swimmer is in front of the therapist, facing away and supported by a bicycle forearm hold (p. 55)	As primary, but the hold is changed to a bicycle fist hold (p. 55)	As primary, but the hold is changed to a bicycle thumb hold (p. 55)
Instruction	'Bend your knees up to your chest and make your legs go round and round like riding a bicycle.' As the swimmer moves the legs the therapist walks around. Both swimmer and therapist sing the nursery rhyme 'The grand old Duke of York'. At this stage of the activity it is inadvisable to lift the swimmer out of the water when singing 'he marched them up to the top of the hill' as strong control of the head and body is required	As primary. If the swimmer is to be lifted out of the water at the appropriate words, a further instruction to 'keep the head forward' must be given	As primary and intermediate. Lifts above the surface of the water can be made higher, thereby demanding greater head and body control to keep the body vertical in a 'ball' in both the buoyancy- and gravity-dominated situations

'HERE WE GO LOOBY LOO' OR 'THE HOKEY COKEY'

A 'ball' and 'stick' activity.

The chorus and first verse used for this activity are as follows:

Chorus:
Here we go Looby Loo
Here we go Looby Li
Here we go Looby Loo
All on a Saturday night.

1st verse:
I put my right arm in
I put my right arm out
I shake it a little, a little
And turn myself about.

Therapeutic aims

1. To encourage and improve balance and co-ordination.
2. To improve body image, spatial awareness and laterality.
3. To develop head and trunk rotation.
4. To improve respiration and breathing control.
5. To increase mental adaptability.

'Here we go Looby Loo' or 'The Hokey Cokey'

	Primary activity	*Intermediate activity*	*Advanced activity*
Purpose	Vertical rotation, lateral rotation in the vertical plane; laterality; turbulent effect	As primary	As primary
Appreciation	The effect of head movement on the body; body image; right and left	As primary	As primary
Formation	The swimmer is in front of the therapist, facing away. The holds vary throughout the activity (see bicycle hold, p. 55)	As primary, but the hold is changed to a bicycle fist hold (see p. 55), and less support is given when performing the actions of the arms and turning	As primary, but the hold is changed to a bicycle thumb hold and no support is given when performing the arm and leg actions and turning
Instruction (same for all three activities)	Varies from verse to verse. *Chorus* (see p. 114): using a forearm bicycle hold, the circle of swimmers and therapists moves round in one direction, the swimmers flexing and extending the legs as if riding a bicycle, and using the head to maintain the vertical position. *1st verse* (see p. 114): the swimmers and therapists face into the circle and the hold is changed to the waist. The swimmers follow the action in the verse, but if unable to turn themselves about, the therapist either 'turns about' with them or facilitates the turn. The chorus is repeated in between every other verse. The actions follow according to the verse that is being used, i.e. *2nd verse*: 'I put my left arm in', *3rd verse*: 'I put my right foot in', *4th verse*: 'I put my left foot in', *5th verse*: 'I put my whole self in'		

'THE WHEELS OF THE BUS'

A 'ball' and 'stick' activity mainly suitable for a group.

1st verse:
The wheels of the bus go round and round,
round and round, round and round
The wheels of the bus go round and round
Down the busy street.

2nd verse:
The people on the bus go up and down,
up and down, up and down.
The people on the bus go up and down
Down the busy street.

3rd verse:
The driver on the bus goes toot toot toot,
toot toot toot, toot toot toot
The driver on the bus goes toot toot toot
Down the busy sreet

4th verse:
The windscreen wipers go swish swish swish
swish swish swish, swish swish swish
The windscreen wipers go swish swish swish
Down the busy street

As an alternative and to introduce further appreciation of vertical and lateral rotation, lateral sway and drag effect, the following form may be used.

A circle is formed by alternate swimmer and therapist using a short arm hold. The swimmers are instructed to sit in their chairs and put their heads back slowly until lying out long. The circle of therapists then moves round in waterwheel fashion. As the verse finishes, the swimmers are instructed to 'recover forwards', that is, to bend the knees up to the chest, heads forward, blow and stand up.

Therapeutic aims

1. To improve head control antero-posteriorly.
2. To encourage active movement of the limbs, and flexion of the body as a whole.
3. To develop head and trunk rotation.
4. To increase balance and co-ordination.
5. To develop control of upper limbs.
6. To improve respiration and breathing control.
7. To increase mental adaptability.
8. To improve body image and spatial awareness.

'The wheels of the bus'

	Primary activity	*Intermediate activity*	*Advanced activity*
Purpose	Vertical rotation; body image; spatial relationships; lateral rotation in the vertical plane	As primary	As primary
Appreciation	The effect of head movement on the body; awareness of body parts and the body in space	As primary	As primary
Formation	Varies from verse to verse	As primary, but a bicycle fist hold is used and less support and assistance given to any of the actions. If the waterwheel formation is used, the hold would change to a long arm hold	As primary, but the bicycle thumb hold is used and little or no support is given in the other formations. In the final verse, if a waterwheel formation is used, the wheel could change directions and a kicking action of the legs be introduced
Instruction (same for all three activities)	*1st verse* (see p. 116): the swimmer is in front and facing away from the therapist, who is using a bicycle forearm hold. A circle of swimmers and therapists moves around 'bicycling' and singing. *2nd verse* (see p. 116): the swimmers and therapists turn to face the middle of the circle. The therapist supports the swimmer at the waist, while the swimmers jump up and down rhythmically, blowing as they come down towards the water. *3rd verse* (see p. 116): the swimmers and therapists turn a face in one direction, using the bicycle forearm hold. As the words 'toot toot toot' are sung and the swimmer brings the head forward and blows into the water, the circle moves round. *4th verse* (see p. 116): the swimmers and therapists face into the middle of the circle. The swimmer is instructed to clasp the outstretched hands together while the therapist supports at the waist. The swimmer then moves the arms through the water from side to side. *5th verse*: This is a repeat of the 1st verse, and the actions can be the same.		

'THE RED RED ROBIN'

A 'ball' and 'stick' activity suitable for a group.

Therapeutic aims

1. To develop rotational control in an anterior/posterior direction, including head control.
2. To improve body image and spatial awareness.
3. To develop balance and co-ordination.
4. To improve respiration and breathing control.
5. To increase mental adaptability.
6. To increase range of movement, especially abduction/adduction.
7. To increase active flexion/extension of the body as a whole.

'The red red robin'

	Primary action	*Intermediate action*	*Advanced action*
Purpose	Vertical rotational control	As primary	As primary
Appreciation	The effect of head movement on the body	As primary	As primary
Formation	A circle is formed with alternate swimmer and therapist using a short arm hold	As primary, but a long arm hold is used	As intermediate
Instruction	'Bend your knees, put your head back and let your legs come up and lie out long. We will all sing "The red red robin" and when we say "get up, get out of bed", bend your knees up to your chest, bring your head forward, blow and stand up.'	As primary	As primary but 'Now we are going to walk sideways, slowly lie back and stand up as before, then continue walking'. The circle moves round and the swimmers have to control vertical rotation on the move. Some lateral rotational control in the horizontal is introduced when the swimmers are lying supine and being moved round in the circle by the therapists

OVER THE ARCHES

A 'ball' and 'stick' activity suitable for a group. It may be used in conjunction with 'Under the arches'.

Therapeutic aims

1. To encourage movement, balance and co-ordination.
2. To develop body image and spatial awareness.
3. To develop and maintain head control.
4. To improve respiration and breathing control.
5. To increase the range of flexion/extension in the body as a whole.
6. To increase mental adaptability.
7. To improve gait.

	Primary activity	*Intermediate activity*	*Advanced activity*
Purpose	Vertical rotation, head control and extremes of posture	As primary	As primary
Appreciation	The effect of head movement on the body	As primary	As primary
Formation	A circle of alternate swimmer and therapist using a long arm hold	As primary	As primary

Over the arches

Instruction	This is continued throughout the activity to encourage the correct action. At no time is there a break in the holds around the circle. One swimmer is asked to walk forward across the circle to the other side, where a swimmer's and therapist's arms are making an arch just below the surface of the water. The swimmer is then instructed to 'sit', put the head back slowly and lie out long. The therapists on either side 'push' the swimmer over the arch. Once over the arch, the swimmer is instructed to curl up into a ball and stand up. The actions of 'ball' and 'stick' are repeated as the swimmer goes backwards over the arch and stands up, assisted by the therapists, when all walk backwards to the original position. 'Keep our head forward and stick your seat out when walking backwards in water.' This activity is repeated by each child in the group	As primary. To increase the difficulty, this activity can be done more rapidly and with less assistance for the swimmer	As intermediate

UNDER THE ARCHES

A 'ball' and 'stick' activity suitable for a group. It can be used in conjunction with 'Over the arches'.

Therapeutic aims

1. To encourage movement, balance and co-ordination.
2. To develop body image and spatial awareness.
3. To improve and maintain head control.
4. To improve respiration and breathing control.
5. To increase active flexion/extension in the body as a whole.
6. To increase mental adaptability.
7. To improve gait.

Under the arches

	Primary activity	*Intermediate activity*	*Advanced activity*
Purpose	Upthrust, rotational control, mental adaptability	As primary	As primary
Appreciation	Buoyancy of the water	As primary	As primary
Formation	A circle of swimmers and therapists is placed alternately using a long arm hold	As primary	As primary
Instruction	Without a break in the circle, a swimmer walks across the circle to 'duck' under the arch made by a swimmer and therapist's arms just below the surface. The swimmer is instructed to 'bend the knees', go under the arch blowing and stand up on the other side. The therapists continue to hold the swimmers' hands throughout the action. To return into the circle, the swimmer bends the knees and comes backwards under the arch blowing, standing up prior to walking backwards to the original position	As primary. The progressions are made by lowering the level of the arch and finally allowing the swimmer to perform the activity independently	As intermediate

WALKING IN SPACE

A 'stick' activity suitable for a group or an individual.

This activity can be progressed even further by increasing the rocking action, the speed and thereby the turbulent effects. This demands greater head control, increased ability to hold the therapist and/ or move around the therapist without holding. In the latter instance the swimmer is paddling independently.

Therapeutic aims

1. To encourage and maintain head control.
2. To encourage movement of head, trunk, upper and lower limbs.
3. To encourage balance and co-ordination.
4. To improve respiration and breathing control.
5. To increase mental adaptability.
6. To improve spatial awareness.

Walking in space

	Primary activity	*Intermediate activity*	*Advanced activity*
Purpose	Vertical and lateral control in the vertical	As primary	As primary
Appreciation	The effect of head movement on the body	As primary	As primary
Formation	The swimmer in front of the therapist, facing away. A hold for lateral rotation in the vertical plane is used (p. 59)	*Phase 1*: As primary but the therapist now rocks from side to side *Phase 2*: As primary and phase 1, but the therapist also moves sideways *Phase 3*: As primary and phases 1 and 2. If the child circles the therapist in a clockwise direction, the therapist then pivots counterclockwise on the longitudinal body axis	As primary and intermediate phases 1, 2 and 3, but the therapist now turns in the same direction as that taken by the swimmer when proceeding out of the arms and around the therapist
Instruction	'Turn round and face me. Touch the side of my head with one arm to open the doors. Turn round and face out of the doors. "Walk" down my arms and out and around my back. Walk up my arms and close the doors by touching the other side of my head. Turn around and face away from me.'	As primary	As primary

'LITTLE BOATS ARE ON THE SEA'

A combined 'ball' and 'stick' activity suitable for a group, but which can be adapted for individual work. The song is taken from *This Little Puffin — Nursery Songs and Rhymes* (Matterson, 1969).

Therapeutic aims

1. To improve head control.
2. To encourage flexion and extension of the body as a whole.
3. To improve and maintain respiration and breathing control.
4. To develop awareness of body image, the extremes of posture and the body in space.
5. To improve mental adaptability.

'Little boats are on the sea'

	Primary activity	*Intermediate activity*	*Advanced activity*
Purpose	Vertical rotational control	As primary	As primary
Appreciation	The effect of movement of the head on the body	As primary	As primary
Formation	The swimmer is in front of the therapist, supported as in the back lying hold (p. 55)	A circle is formed with alternate swimmer and therapist using a short arm hold (p. 57)	As intermediate, except that the hold is changed to a long arm hold (p. 57)
Instruction	'Lie still and relaxed until we sing "loudly the wind begins to shout", then bend your knees to your chest, head and hands forwards, blow and stand up. As the wind dies away, lie back again.'	'Swimmers, bend your knees, head back slowly and lie out long.' The therapists move the circle two or three steps in one direction and then in the other until the words 'loudly the wind', when the swimmers recover to the vertical and blow, lying back again as the wind dies and the circle continues moving	As intermediate. As the swimmer progresses, the speed and tossing movements can be increased. At all times the therapist must observe the swimmer's recovery action for the correct components of movement

LATERAL ROTATION — VERTICAL PLANE

The following activities are primarily concerned with lateral rotation in the vertical plane and follow sequentially. Partial lateral rotation in vertical may already have been introduced in activities such as 'The wheels of the bus' during the windscreen wiper section, and in 'Here we go Looby Loo', for example, a complete turn has taken place. This turning action in the upright can be further developed in the ensuing activities (Table 5b).

PASSING THE RING

A 'stick' activity suitable for a group and which must be played in both clockwise and counter-clockwise directions.

Objects such as balls, fish or ducks may be used instead of the ring. Where manipulation is difficult or impossible, the object can be made to move on to the next swimmer by turbulence. In this case the swimmer rotates the body towards the next swimmer, and the object which has been floating on the opposite side will be drawn across by the turbulent effect.

As the swimmer's control of lateral rotation improves, this activity can also be played in the supine lying position, when it is advanced in the same manner as described on p. 129. The critical element is the ability of the swimmer to roll the body in both directions using the head and limbs. Finally, the swimmer will be able to perform a complete 360° roll independently, and for this the following activity may be used.

Therapeutic aims

1. To improve and maintain head and trunk rotation.
2. To improve laterality, body image and spatial awareness.
3. To improve balance and co-ordination.
4. To improve control of the limbs.
5. To improve respiration and breathing control.

Table 5b Activities for the development of rotational control

Lateral rotation — vertical plane

1. Walking in space
2. Passing the ring
3. This is the way we roll around
4. Turning in the circle
5. Jumping on the spot

Lateral rotation — horizontal plane

1. Seaweed	6. Passing the ring (see vertical plane)
2. Hallo	7. Rolling arm to arm
3. Rolling on to the bar	8. Rolling through 360°
4. Resisted rolling	9. Rolling around the circle
5. The wheel	

Passing the ring

	Primary activity	*Intermediate activity*	*Advanced activity*
Purpose	Lateral rotational control in the vertical plane	As primary	As primary
Appreciation	The effect of turning the head and taking the arm across the body on the body position	As primary	As primary
Formation	The swimmer stands in front of the therapist, supported at the waist, facing into the circle	As primary, but the circle is widened a little	As intermediate, but the circle is widened further
Instruction	'Pass the ring which is in your right hand across the body to the swimmer on your left and look at them. Once the ring has been taken from your hand, turn your head back in the opposite direction until your body is in a flat position.'	As primary	As primary. At no time must the swimmer change the ring from one hand to the other in front of the body. Such action defeats the purpose of the activity

'THIS IS THE WAY WE ROLL AROUND'

A 'stick' activity suitable for a group.

Therapeutic aims

1. To encourage head control.
2. To improve balance and co-ordination.
3. To develop rotation around the longitudinal axis of the body.
4. To improve body image and spatial awareness.
5. To increase mental adaptability.
6. To improve respiration and breathing control.

'This is the way we roll around'

	Primary activity	*Intermediate activity*	*Advanced activity*
Purpose	Lateral rotation in the vertical and horizontal positions	As primary	As primary
Appreciation	Effect of turning the head on the body	As primary	As primary
Formation	The child stands in front of the therapist facing into the middle of the circle	As primary	The child lies supine on the therapist's hands, feet into the middle of the circle
Instruction	'Turn around and face your therapist. Now turn and face into the circle again, singing "This is the way we turn around, turn around, turn around. This is the way we turn around, when in the pool we play".' This can be progressed to a complete turn in front of the therapist	'Jump right round in front of your therapist, turning your head and taking an arm across your body.' In jumping and turning to the right, the left arm is taken across the body. The jump can be started in half turns and progressed to the full turn. Watch that the swimmer blows, singing as above	'Half roll to the right and back flat.' Repeat to the left, singing as in primary. This is progressed to a complete roll in front of the therapist or can be used to roll around the circle from therapist to therapist as in 'Rolling round the circle'

TURNING IN THE CIRCLE

A 'stick' game suitable for a group.

Therapeutic aims

1. To develop rotation of the head and trunk.
2. To improve control of the limbs.
3. To encourage movement, balance and co-ordination.
4. To increase mental adaptability.
5. To improve respiration and breathing control.

Turning in the circle

	Primary activity	*Intermediate activity*	*Advanced activity*
Purpose	Lateral rotational control in the vertical plane	As primary	As primary
Appreciation	The effect of turning the head on the body with upper limb involvement	As primary	As primary
Formation	The swimmers stand with their hands on the therapists' shoulders in a face-to-face position. The therapists complete the circle formation by using a long arm hold with each other	As primary	As primary
Instruction	'You are all going to walk and turn all round the circle. Take your right hand off the shoulder and in to the middle of the circle and continue to take it back and out towards the next therapist's left shoulder. Let go with your left hand and bring it round to the therapist's right shoulder so that you are facing a new therapist.' This rotatory action is repeated right round the circle and performed in the opposite direction	As primary but 'Now you must only use your fingertips to touch the shoulders.'	'This time take your feet off the bottom as you rotate round the circle and hold as lightly as you can.' At this level the swimmers are rotating at an angle of 45°

JUMPING ON THE SPOT

A 'stick' activity suitable for individual or group work.

Therapeutic aims

1. To develop rotation of head and trunk and encourage active movement.
2. To improve and maintain balance and co-ordination.
3. To improve respiration and breathing control.
4. To encourage control of the upper and lower limbs.
5. To increase mental adaptability.

Jumping on the spot

	Primary activity	*Intermediate activity*	*Advanced activity*
Purpose	Lateral rotation in the vertical plane	As primary	As primary
Appreciation	The effect on the body of turning the head	As primary	As primary
Formation	The swimmer stands back to front of the therapist and encircled around the chest by the therapist's arms. There is no contact other than that of the swimmer's arms on top of those of the therapist (p. 59)	As primary, but the swimmer is only supported at the waist	As primary, but no support is given to the swimmer
Instruction	'Turn round and say "Hallo" to me; you can use my arms to help you round.' Once the swimmer is facing the therapist, the instruction is to turn and face away again. Turning in both directions must be developed as it is an essential skill for safety	'Jump round and face me', then 'Jump round and face away'. The swimmer must turn the head in the direction of the movement and may also take the arm on the opposite side of the body across the chest to facilitate the jump	'Jump all the way round and face away from me again.' The same action of the head and arm is required and the swimmer must regain a stable position on landing

LATERAL ROTATION — HORIZONTAL PLANE

The following activities take the child from turning in the vertical plane to rotating in the horizontal. A halfway stage is possible if required, and is achieved by the child rotating around the circle of therapists' arms with the feet off the bottom, as in the activity 'Rolling round the circle'.

It should be remembered that the ability to create or control a roll around the longitudinal axis of the body is dependent upon the use of the head and limbs. The activities described below encourage the use of these body parts. In developing the rolling action, the therapist must ensure that the child is able to rotate in both directions, that is, to the right and to the left.

SEAWEED

A 'stick' activity suitable for an individual and a group.

Therapeutic aims

1. To encourage relaxation.
2. To improve balance and co-ordination in the horizontal.
3. To encourage control of upper and lower limbs.

Seaweed

	Primary activity	*Intermediate activity*	*Advanced activity*
Purpose	Lateral rotational control in the horizontal position	As primary	As primary
Appreciation	The effect of lateral sway and drag on the body	As primary	As primary
Formation	The swimmer is supported by the therapist in supine lying, held under the waist	As primary, but less support is given and, provided no adverse response occurs, a widening of the swaying action	As intermediate, but less support is given and the relaxed body of the swimmer is drawn backwards by the turbulence created by the movement of the therapist
Instruction	'Lie still and relax; be like a piece of seaweed floating in the water.' The therapist walks backwards swaying the swimmer from side to side so that the legs and lower trunk relax	As primary	As primary

'HALLO' (Fig. 35)

A 'stick' activity suitable for a group or an individual. It is similar to 'Seaweed'; the differences relate to the swing of the floating body and the turn of the swimmer's head.

Fig. 35 *'Hallo'.*

Therapeutic aims

1. To improve and maintain head control and rotation of the cervical spine.
2. To improve and maintain balance and co-ordination.
3. To improve respiration and breathing control.
4. To increase body awareness, especially of the lower limbs.

'Hallo'

	Primary activity	*Intermediate activity*	*Advanced activity*
Purpose	Lateral rotational control in the horizontal plane	As primary	As primary
Appreciation	The effect of lateral sway and the drag of the body; the effect of head turning on the body	As primary	As primary
Formation	The swimmer is supported by the therapist in supine lying, held at the waist	As primary, but the speed of the swing from side to side is increased	As primary and intermediate, with increasing speed and swing
Instruction	'When you are swayed out to the side, turn your head and say "Hallo" to me.' The therapist walks backwards, swaying the swimmer from side to side so that the arms are extended and the swimmer's body is at arm's length from the therapist	As primary	As primary. The therapist requires the development of head turning independently of the rest of the body as a means of creating and controlling lateral rotation

ROLLING ON TO THE BAR

A 'stick' activity suitable for a group or individual. It is a progression from the 'Seaweed' and 'Hallo' activities and can be incorporated in them and others which involve the supine lying position and movement through the water, such as 'Speedboats'.

Therapeutic aims

1. To encourage movement in rotational pattern for head, trunk and limbs, and control of the head and limbs.
2. To reduce truncal spasticity.
3. To improve respiration and breathing control.
4. To improve balance and co-ordination.
5. To increase mental adaptability.
6. To increase body image and spatial awareness.

Rolling on to the bar

	Primary activity	*Intermediate activity*	*Advanced activity*
Purpose	Lateral rotational control in the horizontal plane	As primary	As primary
Appreciation	The effect of turning the head on the body	As primary	As primary
Formation	The swimmer is supported by the therapist in supine lying, held under the waist	As primary, but less assistance is given in creating the roll on to the bar and greater speed encouraged	As intermediate, but no assistance is given to creating the roll on to the bar
Instruction	'Relax and let me sway you through the water. When we reach the other side of the pool, turn your head to the left, reach for the bar with your right hand, then your left hand, bring your legs up underneath you and stand up.' If the swimmer rolls to the right, the head is turned in that direction and the left hand reaches for the bar first	As primary	As primary

RESISTED ROLLING

A 'stick' activity suitable for group or individual.

Therapeutic aims

1. To develop, maintain and improve cervical rotation.
2. To create a change in shape, especially when extension is required on one side of the body.
3. To improve co-ordination.
4. To encourage mental adaptability.

Resisted rolling

	Primary activity	*Intermediate activity*	*Advanced activity*
Purpose	Lateral rotational control in the supine lying position	As primary	As primary
Appreciation	The effect of the movement of the head on the body	As primary	As primary
Formation	The swimmer stands in front of the therapist, facing away. The backing hold for the vertical position is used by the therapist (pp. 54 and 55)	As primary	As primary
Instruction	'Sit in the chair, hands forwards, put your head back on my shoulder and let your legs go out long.' 'When you are rolled to the left, turn your head to the right and feel how your body comes flat again.' 'If you are rolled to the right, turn your head to the left to bring the body flat.' The therapist rolls the swimmer manually, first to one side and then to the other, and allows the body of the swimmer to return to the supine lying position when the swimmer turns the head away from the roll	As primary. The therapist gives resistance to the uppermost side of the swimmer's body and prevents, to some degree, a return to the flat position. The swimmer has to work harder in turning the head and extends and abducts along the side of the body to which the head is now turned	As intermediate. Progression is brought about by increasing the amount of resistance given to the counter-rotational action

THE WHEEL (Fig. 36)

A 'stick' activity suitable for a group.

Therapeutic aims

1. To improve balance and co-ordination.
2. To increase and maintain mental adaptability.

Fig. 36 *'Water wheel' formation using a long arm hold. A short arm hold may also be employed.*

The wheel

	Primary activity	*Intermediate activity*	*Advanced activity*
Purpose	Lateral rotational control in the horizontal	As primary	As primary
Appreciation	The effect of movement of the head on the position of the body	As primary	As primary
Formation	A circle is formed with the swimmers and therapists placed alternately, using a short arm hold (p. 57)	As primary, except that the short arm hold is changed to a long arm hold (p. 57)	As intermediate
Instruction	'Swimmers, bend your knees and hips and sit; put your heads back slowly and lie out full length.' The therapists then walk sideways in one direction and the swimmers relax and allow their bodies to be moved through the water. When the therapists change the direction of the circle, the legs of the swimmers will tend to swing away from the centre of the 'wheel'. The swimmer is then instructed to turn the head to prevent this lateral movement of the legs and feet	As primary. The progression is achieved by the change of hold and more frequent alterations in direction of the circle	As intermediate, with further progression achieved by increasing the speed and frequency of the changes in direction

ROLLING ARM TO ARM

A 'stick' activity suitable for groups and individuals.

Therapeutic aims

1. To develop rotation of head and trunk.
2. To develop control of the limbs.
3. To improve balance and co-ordination.
4. To improve respiratory and breathing control.
5. To increase body image and spatial awareness.

Rolling arm to arm

	Primary activity	*Intermediate activity*	*Advanced activity*
Purpose	Lateral rotation in the horizontal	As primary	As primary
Appreciation	The effect of rotation of the head on the body	As primary	As primary
Formation	The hold is described on p. 58	As primary	As primary
Instruction	'Turn your head towards me; bring your outer arm over my arm and the outer leg across the other; blow as you roll.' The position of the swimmer above the surface of the water as the roll occurs can be controlled by the therapist. At first the head and shoulders are above the surface. The finishing position after each roll is on the opposite arm of the therapist so that from which the roll was commenced. After each roll, the swimmer's leading arm will be behind the therapist's shoulders	As primary. Progression is achieved by providing less assistance and allowing the roll to occur lower in the water	As primary. Progression is achieved by allowing the roll to occur virtually unaided at the surface. Any suitable rhythmical music may be used to develop the rolling action

ROLLING THROUGH 360°

A 'stick' activity suitable for individual work, but a group could be formed with each therapist working with a swimmer. The movement can be taught with an extension or flexion pattern according to the condition of the swimmer.

Therapeutic aims

1. To improve head control.
2. To encourage active movement.
3. To increase mental adaptability.
4. To reduce muscle spasm in the trunk through the rhythmical rotatory action.
5. To improve respiration and breathing control.
6. To improve balance and co-ordination.

Rolling through 360°

	Primary activity	*Intermediate activity*	*Advanced activity*
Purpose	Lateral rotation in the horizontal	As primary	As primary
Appreciation	The effect of head, arm and leg movement on the body	As primary	As primary
Formation	Swimmer lying horizontal beside the therapist who uses the second rolling hold (p. 58)	As primary	As primary
Instruction	'Bring your outer arm and leg across your body; turn your head towards me; blow as you roll and lift on the elbow of the other arm as you come round.' The therapist pats the waist of the swimmer to facilitate the action	As primary. The progression is obtained by the therapist giving less assistance	As primary. Little or no support is provided by the therapist. Independent rolling through 360° in both directions should be possible at this stage. It is important that all rolling should be carried out rhythmically

ROLLING ROUND THE CIRCLE

A 'stick' activity suitable for a group.

The rolling action must be developed to both the right and left. Most swimmers have a preferred direction but, in the interests of safety, must learn to create and control lateral rotation in both directions.

Therapeutic aims

1. To develop rotational patterns of head, trunk and limbs, encouraging creation and control of rotation.
2. To reduce truncal spasticity.
3. To encourage active movement.
4. To improve and maintain respiration and breathing control.
5. To increase body image and spatial awareness.

	Primary activity	*Intermediate activity*	*Advanced activity*
Purpose	Lateral rotational control in the horizontal plane	As primary	As primary
Appreciation	The effect of creating a roll and controlling the body when rolling	As primary	As primary
Formation	The swimmer stands in front of the therapist, facing into the circle	As primary, except that the circle is widened a little	As intermediate, with further widening of the circle
Instruction	'Bend your knees, hands forward, head back slowly until you are floating.' The therapist gives support at the waist to stabilise the swimmer's floating position. 'You are rolling to the left. When the instruction "roll" is given, turn your head to the left and bring your right arm and leg across your body, blow, and roll on to the next therapist.' As the swimmer leaves the therapist's hands, the therapist prepares to receive the next swimmer. It is advisable to wait at this point until all swimmers have completed the roll and are lying in the supine position on the hands of the next therapist	As primary. A suitable song may be introduced to develop a more rhythmical pattern of rolling as well as to control the timing of each roll. The therapists give less and less support to the swimmers	As primary and intermediate. Assistance is only given when required

COMBINED ROTATION

Combined rotation is concerned with linking vertical and lateral rotation to ensure the swimmer's safety. The combination of the two rotational movements permits a swimmer to fall forwards, turn on to the back and recover forward again to the upright position if desired (Table 5c).

Table 5c Activities for the development of rotational control

Combined rotation
1. In and out the windows
2. Mushroom float
3. Beyond the vertical
4. Fishes in the net

IN AND OUT THE WINDOWS

A 'ball' and 'stick' activity suitable for a group.

Therapeutic aims

1. To increase mental adaptability.
2. To improve respiration and breathing control.
3. To improve balance and co-ordination.
4. To encourage active and independent movement.
5. To increase spatial awareness and directionality.

In and out the windows

	Primary activity	*Intermediate activity*	*Advanced activity*
Purpose	Lateral rotation and upthrust	As primary	As primary
Appreciation	The effect of head movement on the body to produce rotation and upthrust effects	As primary	As primary
Formation	Swimmers holding hands in a line inside the circle formed by the therapists who hold each other's hands to form arches at the surface of the water	As primary	The swimmers do not hold hands
Instruction	'Follow the leader under the arch; come up outside the circle and move on to another arch. Go under the arch coming inside the circle. Move all the way round the circle and don't forget to follow.'	As primary, but 'The circle is going to move round slowly so watch for the arches.'	As primary, but 'Do not hold hands this time.'

MUSHROOM FLOAT

A 'ball' activity suitable for individual activity, but a group of swimmers and therapists may be formed. It is a prerequisite for combined rotation and the appreciation of upthrust.

Therapeutic aims

1. To improve flexion and extension of the body as a whole.
2. To increase respiration and breathing control.
3. To improve mental adaptability.
4. To improve balance and co-ordination.

Mushroom float

	Primary activity	*Intermediate activity*	*Advanced activity*
Purpose	Combined rotation and upthrust	As primary	As primary
Appreciation	The effects of upthrust and the value of rotational control	As primary	As primary
Formation	The swimmer stands in front of the therapist, facing away. Support is given at the swimmer's waist by the therapist	As primary	As primary
Instruction	'Bend your knees up to your chest; hold your knees with your hands, head forward and blow.' The therapist controls the forward action of the body that will occur as the 'ball' shape is achieved, so that the swimmer's body does not rotate forwards too rapidly	As primary. Progression is achieved by the lessening of the support and control provided by the therapist	As primary, but stress that the flexion of hips and knees should be performed slowly to aid flotation. No assistance is given to the swimmer by the therapist

BEYOND THE VERTICAL

A 'stick and ball' activity suitable for individual work which can be performed in a group.

Therapeutic aims

1. To improve flexion, extension and rotation of the body as a whole.
2. To improve head control.
3. To increase respiration and breathing control.
4. To improve mental adaptability.
5. To increase balance and co-ordination.

Beyond the vertical

	Primary activity	*Intermediate activity*	*Advanced activity*
Purpose	Combined rotational control	As primary	As primary
Appreciation	The importance of rotational control for recovering to a safe breathing position and restoring balance	As primary	As primary
Formation	Swimmer stands in front of the therapist, facing away. Support is given at the swimmer's waist	As primary	As primary
Instruction	'Sit in your chair with your hands forward; put your head back slowly and lie out long. Bend your knee up to your chest, head and hands forward; blow, and go forward beyond the upright position. Then turn on to your back and recover forwards to me.'	As primary. Less facilitation and support is given. The therapist should be the focal point to which the swimmer recovers after rotating in the horizontal	As primary. Objects floating on the water or under the water can be retrieved by the swimmer and presented to the therapist. This will encourage greater movement and provides interest in the activity

FISHES IN THE NET

A 'ball' and 'stick' activity for a group.

Therapeutic aims

1. To maintain rotational control, balance and co-ordination.
2. To improve respiration and breathing control.
3. To encourage active movement throughout the body in all directions.
4. To increase body image and spatial awareness.
5. To improve mental adaptability.

Fishes in the net

	Primary activity	*Intermediate activity*	*Advanced activity*
Purpose	Combined rotation	As primary	As primary
Appreciation	The effects of buoyancy; rotational control and the combination of vertical and lateral rotation required to gain a safe breathing position	As primary	As primary
Formation	A circle is formed by the therapists using a long arm hold (p. 58) around the swimmers who stand independently in the middle of the circle	As primary	As primary
Instruction	'Swimmers, you are fishing in the net and you can get out of the net by going under the arms, and come back in over them. You can hold the arms to assist you if you wish.' The swimmers proceed out of the circle under the arms and, once clear, rotate onto the back and recover to the upright position. This pattern is repeated as the swimmers return into the circle	As primary, but the swimmers must not use the therapists' arms to assist exit and entry of the circle	As primary, but the circle is going to move round in one direction or the other and may change from time to time. The skill of keeping the eyes open under water is also encouraged since the swimmers must watch for the spaces to exit and enter the circle

UPTHRUST

Activities in this section are designed to help the swimmer appreciate the effects of buoyancy or upthrust. The swimmer is encouraged to go to the bottom of the pool, which is difficult due to upthrust effects. True appreciation of these effects reassures the swimmer, and a change of attitude develops when it is clearly understood that water acts as an upward force rather than a downward one (Table 5d).

Table 5d Activities for the development of rotational control

Upthrust
1. The big ship sails through the alley alley O
2. Oranges and lemons
3. Pieces of eight
4. Sitting on the bottom

'THE BIG SHIP SAILS THROUGH THE ALLEY ALLEY O'

A 'stick' and 'ball' activity suitable for group work.

'The big ship sails through the Alley Alley O,
Alley Alley O, Alley Alley O;
The big ship sails through the Alley Alley O,
On the last day of September.

The captain said "It will never, never do,
Never, never do, never, never do,"
The captain said "It will never, never do,"
On the last day of September.

The big ship sank to the bottom of the sea,
The bottom of the sea, the bottom of the sea,
The big ship sank to the bottom of the sea,
On the last day of September.

We all dip our heads in the deep blue sea,
The deep blue sea, the deep blue sea,
We all dip our head in the deep blue sea,
On the last day of September.'

Therapeutic aims

1. To improve respiration and breathing control.
2. To increase mental adaptability.
3. To improve head control in the anterior/posterior direction.
4. To encourage flexion and extension of the body as a whole.
5. To encourage independent walking.
6. To increase balance and co-ordination.

'The big ship sails through the Alley Alley O'

	Primary activity	*Intermediate activity*	*Advanced activity*
Purpose	Upthrust control and vertical rotation	As primary	As primary
Appreciation	The effect of head movement on the body and the effects of upthrust	As primary	As primary
Formation	The swimmer in front of the therapist, facing away. A backing waist hold (or, in severely disabled cases, sitting on the therapist's lap, p. 54) is used	The swimmer faces the therapist using a hands on hands hold, the therapist walks backwards	The swimmer now proceeds independently. The therapist is close by if help is required
Instruction	The pairs follow the leader through the Alley O (i.e. a therapist making an arch with the arms towards the side of the pool, or two people hold hands facing each other). The swimmer blows going under the arch. Repeat instruction for second verse	As 'The big ship sank to the bottom of the sea', swimmer and therapist submerge to the bottom, moving under the arch. Also during the fourth verse	The swimmer passes under the arch independently. The therapist can at first be on the other side of the arch to receive the swimmer

'ORANGES AND LEMONS'

(Fig. 37)

A 'stick' and 'ball' activity suitable for a group.

Therapeutic aims

1. To improve respiration and breathing control.
2. To encourage general relaxation.
3. To encourage movement, especially total flexion and extension.
4. To improve and maintain balance and co-ordination.
5. To improve head control, especially in the anterior/posterior direction.

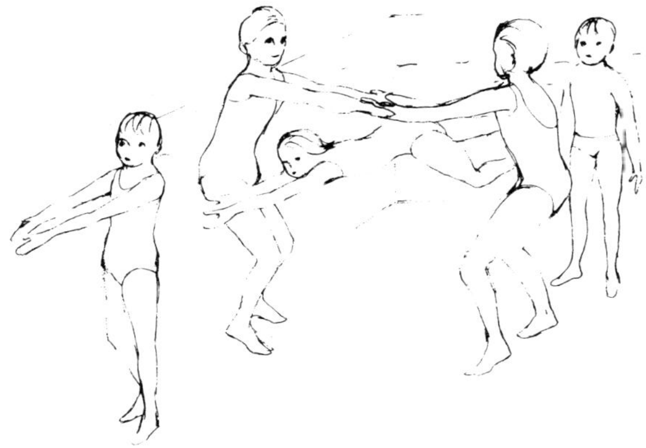

Fig. 37 *Swimming through underarms.*

	Primary activity	*Intermediate activity*	*Advanced activity*
Purpose	Breathing control and upthrust	As primary	As primary
Appreciation	The need for breathing out when submerging; buoyancy effects	As primary	As primary
Formation	One swimmer and therapist make an arch with both arms just below the surface. Other swimmers are supported at the waist, facing away from their therapist, and follow each other under the arch	As primary	As primary
Instruction	'We're going to sing "Oranges and lemons" as you go under the arch below.' The game of 'Oranges and lemons' can be played as on land or simply modified by going under the arch. The important points are breathing control and the willingness on the part of the child to submerge with the head forward rather than extended. Swimmers and therapists submerge under the arch, surfacing on the other side, and follow the leader to repeat the process	As primary. Less assistance is given at the waist, thus allowing greater appreciation of the upthrust effect; alternatively, the swimmer can be placed behind the therapist	No assistance is given, the child submerging and proceeding under the arms independently. The therapist may move round to the other side of the arch to receive the swimmer

PIECES OF EIGHT

A 'stick' activity more suitable for a group but which may be played between two people.

Therapeutic aims

1. To improve respiration and breathing control.
2. To encourage and maintain balance restoration and rotational control.
3. To encourage movement at the surface and below the water.
4. To develop eye–hand co-ordination.
5. To provide perceptual stimulation aurally.

Pieces of eight

	Primary activity	*Intermediate activity*	*Advanced activity*
Purpose	Buoyancy effects and breathing control	As primary	As primary
Appreciation	The effects of buoyancy	As primary	As primary
Formation	A circle is formed with the swimmer in front of the therapist, who supports the swimmer at the waist	As primary, but less assistance is given to the swimmer	As primary, except the swimmer works independently
Instruction	'When I say "go", you all go under the water for these objects. Don't forget to blow.' The therapist may assist submersion if necessary and aids control of buoyancy and rotational effects	'Wait till I say "go".' The objects are pushed further under before the order 'go' is given. If the objects are of different colours, each colour can be given a number and the swimmers encouraged to go for the objects with the higher points. The therapists keep the score for individual swimmers. However, the important factors are that the swimmer is blowing out under water and keeping the eyes open. A variety of objects, some which sink more slowly than others, should be used	As primary and intermediate, but now the objects are allowed to sink close to or right to the bottom of the pool. This activity can be carried out in other formations or on an individual basis, although in the latter situation, competition cannot be introduced

SITTING ON THE BOTTOM

A 'ball' and 'stick' activity.

Therapeutic aims

1. To encourage extremes of posture, body image and spatial awareness.
2. To improve balance and co-ordination.
3. To improve respiratory control.
4. To increase mental adaptability.

Sitting on the bottom

	Primary activity	*Intermediate activity*	*Advanced activity*
Purpose	Upthrust and rotational control	As primary	As primary
Appreciation	The effects of upthrust	As primary	As primary
Formation	Swimmer and therapist facing each other, the swimmer's hands on the therapist's shoulders. The therapist holds the swimmer's waist	A hands on hands hold is used	A circle of alternate swimmers in therapists' long arm hold can be used as a further progression
Instruction	'We will jump up and down three times and then go under the water blowing. See if I am blowing bubbles.'	As primary	The swimmer submerges independently as in the primary activity

ACTIVITIES FOR BALANCE AND CO-ORDINATION

The development of balance control and co-ordination has already commenced in the activities described in the previous sections. However, the activities in this section (Table 6) may be used specifically to increase balance control and stability against the movement of the water, that of the swimmer, and that of other persons in the water.

In these activities the swimmer can obtain a fine degree of balance control against any disturbing factors and should do so in the standing, sitting, kneeling and lying positions.

Turbulence — a strongly disturbing force — may be used deliberately by the therapist around the swimmer to teach such balance control combined with co-ordination.

Therapeutic aims

1. To encourage active movement, especially abduction, adduction of the legs and arms, and elevation of the arms.
2. To develop flexion and extension of the body as a whole.
3. To improve control.
4. To develop body awareness.
5. To develop balance and co-ordination.
6. To improve respiration and breathing control.

Table 6 Activities for balance and co-ordination

Activities for balance and co-ordination
1. Twinkle, twinkle little star
2. Making waves
3. Stars and stripes
4. Speedboats
5. Roundabouts
6. Turbulence deliberately placed around the swimmer

Activities 1–5 are undertaken in the form of a game. Activity 6 is in the form of a technique that aids the development of balance control.

'Twinkle, twinkle, little star'

a 'stick' activity for younger children in a group or individually.

'Twinkle, twinkle, little star'

	Primary activity	*Intermediate activity*	*Advanced activity*
Purpose	Balance control in the vertical and supine lying positions	As primary	As primary
Appreciation	The effect of the use of the head to control the body position	As primary	As primary
Formation	A circle is formed, all facing inwards, the swimmers in front of the therapists, supported at the waist in the vertical	As primary	As primary
Instruction	'As we sing "Twinkle, twinkle, little star, how I wonder what you are", slowly raise your arms out of the water and over your heads.' 'As we sing "Up above the world so high, like a diamond in the sky", make your arms reach as high and as wide as you can.' 'Wave your hand and wiggle your fingers when we sing "Twinkle, twinkle, little star", and bring your arms down into the water when singing "how I wonder what you are".'	'Lift your arms out of the water as we sing "Twinkle, twinkle, little star". Curl up into a ball and lie back slowly and put your legs out long as we sing "how I wonder what you are, up above the world so high". Spread your arms and legs as wide as you can while singing "like a diamond in the sky". Bring your arms and legs together, curl up and stand erect while singing "Twinkle, twinkle, little star, how I wonder what you are".'	As intermediate. The progression is made by increasing the speed of the activity and by the therapist gradually disengaging the hands

MAKING WAVES

A 'stick' activity suitable for group and individual work. It can be used as an activity on its own or as a component of other games such as 'If you're happy and you know it' or 'Simon says'.

Therapeutic aims

1. To increase the range of movement and muscle strength in the arms and legs.
2. To improve balance and co-ordination.
3. To increase awareness of body image and spatial relationships.

Making waves

	Primary activity	*Intermediate activity*	*Advanced activity*
Purpose	Balance control in the vertical and horizontal positions	As primary	As primary
Appreciation	The effect of the head movement on the body and turbulent or drag effect on the moving limbs	As primary	As primary
Formation	The swimmer stands in front of, and facing away from, the therapist who provides support at the waist. The swimmer's shoulders should be in the water	As primary	As primary
Instruction	'Stretch your arms forward, hands flat, and swing your arms out sideways, then bring them together again.'	'Stretch your arms forwards, the palms of your hands facing each other; swing your arms out sideways and then bring them together again.'	'Stretch your hands forwards, head back on the shoulder and lie out long. Let's make waves with arms and legs going in and out.' Progressions are made by decreasing the support given and by increasing the speed of the activity

STARS AND STRIPES

A 'stick' activity.

Therapeutic aims

1. To improve and maintain the range of abduction/ adduction in the hip and shoulder joints.
2. To encourage control of the limbs.
3. To develop rotational control, balance and co-ordination.
4. To develop body image and spatial awareness.

Stars and stripes

	Primary activity	*Intermediate activity*	*Advanced activity*
Purpose	Balance control in supine lying; lateral rotational control	As primary	As primary
Appreciation	The effects of head control on rotation; buoyancy effects	As primary	As primary
Formation	The swimmer stands in front of the therapist, facing away. The therapist places the hands in readiness to support the swimmer in the supine lying position (p. 55)	As primary, less support and assistance being given to the lying position and to recovery. Increasing the speed of the movement increases the degree of control required	The swimmer is not supported, lying back, floating and recovering independently
Instruction (same for all three activities)	'Sit in your chair with your arms forwards; put your head back slowly until you are lying in bed. Part your arms and legs out and make a star. Close your arms and legs and make a stripe'		

SPEEDBOATS

A 'stick' activity.

A greater degree of rotational control may be introduced by encouraging the swimmer to roll on to the bar (see p. 140) as the side of the pool is reached.

Therapeutic aims

1. To encourage movement and control of the limbs.
2. To encourage head and rotational control.
3. To improve balance and co-ordination.

Speedboats

	Primary activity	*Intermediate activity*	*Advanced activity*
Purpose	Movement and control of the legs leading to independent movement in the supine lying positions, involving rotational control	As primary	As primary
Appreciation	Ability to control rotation during movement through the water	As primary	As primary
Formation	The swimmer stands in front of the therapist, facing away. The swimmer proceeds to lie back on the therapist's hands	As primary, but providing less support	As primary. The therapist only supports if necessary to get flotation in the supine lying position, the swimmer then proceeds independently
Instruction (same for all three activities)	'Kick your legs.' The therapist walks backwards supporting the swimmer during the kicking action. If this activity is played in a group, a line of swimmers facing a wall can be formed and in addition to 'Kick your legs', encouragement to move actively can be given by adding a competitive note: 'Who is the fastest speedboat?'		

ROUNDABOUTS

A 'stick' activity suitable for a group which could be modified for working with an individual.

Therapeutic aims

1. To develop and maintain balance control and co-ordination.
2. To improve and maintain postural reactions.
3. To develop control of the limbs, especially that of the arms.
4. To encourage the development of body and spatial awareness.

Roundabouts

	Primary activity	*Intermediate activity*	*Advanced activity*
Purpose	The development of balance and co-ordination; postural reactions and an increase in mental adaptability	As primary	As primary
Appreciation	Turbulent effects with the consequent loss of balance and the need for head control	As primary	As primary
Formation	The swimmers stand back to back in the middle of the circle formed by the therapists. A hands on hands hold is used for each swimmer	As primary	The therapists form a circle around the swimmers using a long arm hold
Instruction	The swimmers remain standing as the therapists walk sideways round the circle, removing the hands from the first swimmer and picking up the hands of the next swimmer. A beat or number is used in order that all therapists move from one swimmer to the next at the same time and the swimmers are only without support momentarily	As primary, but the moving circle may change direction when instructed and the swimmers are given less support	The circle of therapists walks sideways in one direction and then the other with increasing speed. Each swimmer must stabilise the body against the turbulence and remain balanced, 'sitting' with the head and hands forward, the legs hip width apart, the hips, knees and ankles flexed, the feet on the floor of the pool

TURBULENCE DELIBERATELY PLACED AROUND THE SWIMMER

An activity suitable for individual work.

The progression is made by increasing the amount of turbulence placed around the swimmer. Turbulence may be created in the manner described in the primary activity (p. 179) or may be increased by the movement of the therapist around the swimmer. This movement may be slow and gentle at first but may be gradually increased in speed and thus cause greater turbulent effects. Further progressions are achieved by creating turbulence around the swimmer in sitting, kneeling and supine lying.

Therapeutic aims

1. To improve balance and co-ordination, particularly fine balance.
2. To increase mental adaptability.

Turbulence deliberately placed around the swimmer — the factors are the same for all levels of this activity

Purpose	Balance control and co-ordination
Appreciation	The effects of turbulence on the body and the manner in which control can be acquired
Formation	Swimmer standing facing the therapist
Instruction	'Try to stop me making you fall.' The therapist, using the extended arms, creates gentle turbulence in front of the swimmer. This is done by holding one arm above the other in order that the hands may pass over each other. The hands should be shoulder-width apart and pass laterally to the same distance, crossing in midline and back again. If the action is repeated a number of times, turbulence will build up in front of the swimmer. If the turbulence is created low on the swimmer's body, the resulting loss of balance will occur more rapidly. The therapist may need to instruct the swimmer as to how to control the body balance. When the body is falling forwards, the swimmer should lift the arms forward to shoulder level, keep the head forward and at the same time adopt a sitting posture by flexing the hips and knees, Additional stability is obtained if the legs are abducted to just beyond the width of the hips. Turbulence may also be created in the same manner behind the swimmer. In this case the tendency would be for the swimmer's body to fall forwards. In order to counteract this falling action and to stabilise the body, the swimmer should flex the hips and knees slightly, bringing the head and arms forward. If turbulence is placed behind the swimmer and to one side, the swimmer's body will tend to fall backwards and to rotate to the side on which the turbulence has been placed. To avoid a loss of balance and to maintain a position of stability, the swimmer adopts a sitting position, at the same time taking the head and arms forward and away from the direction in which the body would fall and rotate

DYNAMIC ACTIVITIES

The activities included in this section (Table 7) lead directly on to swimming, and many of them may be found in books and manuals concerned with the teaching of swimming. However, it must be appreciated that such activities have been devised for the able-bodied swimmer and may need modification for the disabled.

The advanced levels of activity in many of the preceding pages are appropriate dynamic activities, and it is not proposed to set out in such detail those activities listed here. Once the swimmer has reached the level of ability to cope with dynamic activity, progression through a series of stages, such as has been developed in the games so far, is not necessary.

Swimming strokes frequently need to be modified for each disabled swimmer, and such modifications are dependent almost entirely on the mobility of the swimmer.

An unorthodox approach to stroke techniques is provided.

Table 7 Dynamic activities

Gliding on turbulence
Pushing off and gliding
Mushroom float
Prone float
Log roll
Corkscrew
Washtub
Somersault forward
Somersault backward
Diving for objects
Rowing boats
Swimming through legs
Swimming

Gliding on turbulence

The swimmer floats supine and is moved through the water on turbulence created by the therapist. In shallow water the turbulence may be created by the arms. In deeper water this may be done by the therapist's legs as the supine position is adopted. At all times the turbulence should be placed under the swimmer's trunk at the lower border of the scapulae. The swimmer should control with the head any rolling action of the body that may occur.

Pushing off and gliding

The swimmer pushes off from the side of the pool in either supine or prone, and glides as far as possible without moving the limbs. The hands may be kept at the sides of the body or extended forwards with the thumbs entwined. The legs should be adducted and extended. At the end of the glide the swimmer adopts the erect position.

Mushroom float

This float is also called the jellyfish float. The swimmer bends the knees to the chest and places the hands on the knees. The body rotates forwards and the swimmer floats with the thoracic spine visible above the surface of the water. The face is immersed and the swimmer should slowly be blowing air out of the mouth. This is a useful skill to acquire as it is a prerequisite for somersaulting and is a simple way in which to progress to prone floating.

Prone float

A prone float requires the swimmer to be face down in the water, the arms and legs extended and abducted, thus making a star shape. This position can be altered in several ways and is helpful in teaching the breast stroke action (see p. 183).

Log roll

The body is fully extended, the arms stretched above the head. The body is rotated on the surface of the water without the use of the limbs.

Corkscrew

The corkscrew action is similar to the log roll, but the arm position is altered, one arm remaining extended above the head, the other held at the side.

Washtub

The body is extended in supine lying on the surface with the arms at the side of it. The knees are drawn up to the chest, the thighs being held vertical and the lower leg parallel to the surface of the water. A flat sculling of the hands at the sides rotates the body through 360°. The head remains steady and the eyes looking upwards throughout the activity.

Somersaults — forward and backward

The ability to somersault is of importance to any swimmer, especially when swimming in the sea. Many disabled people can attain this skill, though in some instances somersaulting in either direction may be physically impossible. In such cases it is important for the person's safety that any modified somersault is built on the necessary basic skills performed automatically, and at an advanced level.

The prerequisites for somersaulting are:

(a) the ability to keep the eyes open under water,
(b) the ability to exhale strongly through the nose,
(c) the ability to perform a mushroom float.

Somersaults may be taught in several ways. The simplest method is for two therapists to assist the swimmer: they stand on either side and provide support with their hands.

Forward somersault

The therapist on the swimmer's right places the right clenched hand for support of the swimmer's right hand, and the left hand is placed palm up under the swimmer's thigh. This is reversed for the therapist on the swimmer's left.

Backward somersault

The therapist on the swimmer's right now places the right hand under the swimmer's shin, while the clenched left hand offers support for the swimmer's hand. Again the position is reversed for the therapist on the swimmer's left.

Alternatively, when two therapists are working with a swimmer, they can link hands; the swimmer holds the arms and creates a somersault around them.

When working on an individual basis with a swimmer, the forward somersault can be facilitated by a hand placed on the back as the swimmer curls up into a ball shape. The other hand is placed under the thighs. A backward somersault may be facilitated by support provided by two clenched hands beneath the centre of balance of the body. As the swimmer's body is curled up and the head extended, the therapist moves the hands upwards and laterally to assist the swimmer's action.

When a swimmer has the ability to prone float with the arms extended beyond the head and can push off and glide, somersaulting independently can be achieved. The swimmer adopts the prone position described, pushes off from the side of the pool and at the end of the glide moves the arms to the abducted position, takes the head downwards at the same time flexing the hips and adopting the tuck position. The body rotates around the shoulder joints, having converted linear velocity into angular velocity. If a swimmer is unable to push off from the side of the pool due to a lack of power in the lower limbs, the therapist holds the legs extended, one hand under the thighs, the other on the soles of the feet, and pushes the swimmer through the water, thus providing the motive power for the glide. The swimmer uses the arm and body actions already described to achieve the somersault.

Diving for objects

This activity is an extension of the game 'Pieces of eight' (see p. 164). Any object that sinks may be recovered, and these can range from items such as bricks, dive rings, discs and sticks, to coins. This action ensures that the eyes remain open underwater, and the swimmer should exhale slowly throughout the time the body is submerged.

Rowing boats

Rowing boats is a team activity and one in which a competitive spirit can be engendered. Two or three swimmers stand behind each other, facing the side of the pool. The person nearest the wall remains standing while the second and third lie back in the water and place their legs around the waist of the person in front. All the swimmers use a bilateral arm back stroke, taking the timing from the first person who has now adopted the supine lying position and kicks with the legs also. The boat tries to reach the other side or end of the pool without sinking.

Swimming through legs (Fig. 38)

This activity can be carried out in both a group and individual situation. When working with a group, either a line or a circle formation may be used. If a circle is formed, the therapists hold hands and stand with their legs wide apart sideways. The swimmer goes under one 'arch' and may pull and push against the therapist's leg to move through and round to the next 'arch'. By keeping the body close to the legs, curling around them, the swimmer may be able to increase the number of 'arches' traversed.

If a line formation is used, the therapists stand with a wide stance at arm's length, one behind the other, all facing in the same direction. The gaps

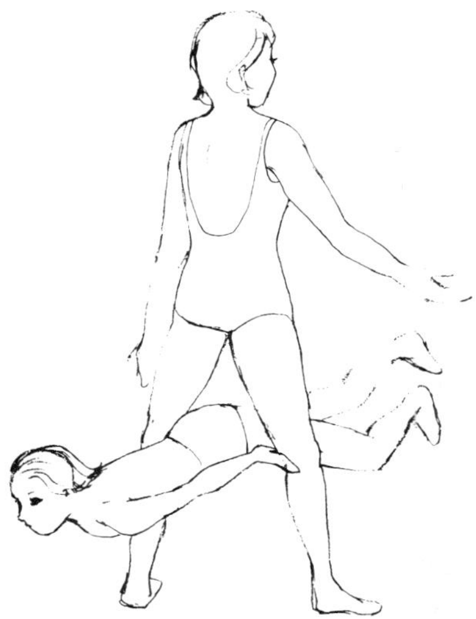

Fig. 38 *Swimming through legs.*

provided allow a swimmer to emerge in between the therapists should the necessity arise.

SWIMMING

Activity in water is considered to be the finest form of exercise for all. For the disabled, water offers an excellent medium for therapeutic exercise and recreation for a wide range of disabilities and for people in any age group. Swimming is a skill that has to be learnt and is the natural progression from water-familiarisation programmes.

Hydrotherapy is the concern of the physiotherapist with a specialised knowledge of disease and disability, of movement and of rehabilitative techniques. However, the teaching of swimming skills has also become part of the therapist's work due to the desirability of the disabled maintaining fitness through recreational activity in water. General teaching techniques and details of specific strokes can be found in books on this subject such as *Swimming: a handbook for teachers* by Helen Elkington (1978).

It must be clearly understood that the application of these methods of teaching swimming strokes is not always successful because allowances for the disability are not made or the handicap understood. Adaptations and modifications are needed and, due to lack of mobility, the strokes produced by a disabled person may not resemble the classic strokes produced by the able-bodied. It seems logical, therefore, to look to a different and less orthodox approach for teaching swimming strokes to the disabled.

The necessity for the acquisition of breathing control has been stressed throughout the text, as well as the important effects it has on relaxation and balance, and the swimmer's breathing ability should be of first concern. This is closely linked with the ability to achieve and maintain safe breathing positions in the water. It is around these points that the swimmer's strokes can be developed. This approach is in contrast to the orthodox method in which the swimmer is taught the technique of the strokes while holding the breath. When the arm and leg actions have been learnt, attempts are made to fit the breathing into the strokes.

There will be certain prerequisites for the various strokes, and these will include the following abilities.

1. To submerge and control exhalation.
2. To keep the eyes open in the interests of safety and in order to swim in a straight direction.
3. To float in both the supine and prone positions.
4. To push off and glide in both the supine and prone positions.
5. To regain and maintain a vertical position from both prone and supine positions.

6. To rotate the body from the supine lying position to prone lying and back to supine again.

Specific strokes will then require the practice of specific actions. These actions vary from stroke to stroke, and the manner in which the progressions may be made is given for back crawl, front crawl and breast stroke. It is advisable to commence with back crawl swimming, for the majority of disabled persons, affected more often and more severely in the lower limbs, can use the upper limbs to maximum advantage to propel the body through the water in the supine position. The face is also clear of the water and any anxiety about breathing is largely removed. This point is reinforced by Elkington (1978), who states that most beginners manage better in the supine position. However, the semi-sitting position, described by her for use initially with disabled persons who have high-floating legs due to loss of density in those limbs, would interfere with the suggestions made below. The high flotation of the lower limbs in cases of spina bifida and paraplegia and the manner in which this may be controlled have already been discussed (see p. 25).

Back crawl stroke

Prerequisite: the ability to back glide, the body extended with toes pointed and the arms by the side.

Training begins with the addition of the leg action, and this is practised to a high level of competence before the arm action is added. During practice with the legs, the arms may be placed in any one of a number of different positions. For example, they can be placed on the abdomen, behind the head with the elbows depressed, held extended above the head with thumbs locked, or folded across the chest.

The leg action also needs to be practised, not only in supine but also in prone and side lying with the arms extended and close to the body. This adds variety and prepares the swimmer for other strokes. When the swimmer is proficient with the leg action, arm movements can be introduced, at first bilaterally simultaneously and then alternating.

In achieving a bilateral movement the swimmer is directed to push backwards, at the same time reaching back 'over the water' with both arms, bringing the hands into the water and pulling strongly under the water back to the side of the body. When reaching back, the arms should be kept low above the surface. When introducing an alternative arm action, the non-reaching arm is inhibited by having the swimmer hold it close to the body. As the swimmer progresses through the water using the leg and *one* arm, the head controls the rolling action of the body. This sequence is repeated with the opposite arm.

When the alternate action of *both* arms is begun,

each arm cycles continuously, moving 'over the water' from the thigh, into the water, and back to the thigh again. The full back crawl (as with all strokes) should initially be practised at a slow pace to reduce errors and conserve energy.

Front crawl stroke

Prerequisites: as for back crawl but with the addition of competence in performing the back crawl stroke.

Gliding in the prone position with the body, arms and legs extended and as flat as possible in the water, is the first action to be practised. This should be repeated frequently at all stages of acquiring the front crawl stroke. The same sequence used in practising the leg action is followed.

It is necessary to introduce breathing control, and initially the swimmer is taught to stop swimming and stand up prior to running out of breath. Later the swimmer is instructed to roll on to the back prior to requiring another breath and to proceed swimming using the back crawl stroke leg action. In the next progression the swimmer lies on the side, with the head turned towards the surface so that the nose and mouth are just clear of the water. The crawl leg action is used to propel the body in this position. It is advisable to commence this lying first on one side and then the other. Once this had been achieved, the swimmer is instructed to lie on one side and extend the arm on that side forward. The other arm is kept close to the body. This is repeated on the other side. The leg action will help to control the balance, but the position of the head is critical. The weight of the head must be taken by the water. Should the swimmer lift the head, the body position is altered to such an extent that all efforts to remain afloat will be sabotaged.

The arm action is introduced as the body moves in the prone glide following the commencement of the leg action. The swimmer moves as far as possible before breathing control is lost and should then stop swimming and stand up. The same sequence used in practising the leg action is followed — that is, the swimmer learns to roll from prone to supine, to breathe, and continues across the width of the pool in this position.

To develop the arm stroke further, the swimmer is instructed to arrest the progression of one arm in full forward extension while the other arm remains at the side. Thus further propulsion is achieved solely by leg action. The arresting procedure alternates between arms and is followed by a slow lazy roll to the side to breathe. The swimmer is told to stay on the side for as long as desired before completing the front crawl stroke with the face in the water. It is now essential that the swimmer learns to keep the arms moving, but turning the head to the left when the left arm is pulling through the water and has reached a point where the hand is immediately below the left shoulder. The face should turn into the water before the hand in its over-water recovery action reaches a line with the shoulder. This is practised in the same manner to the right. It may prove valuable to perform front crawl with continuous leg action, but with only the right arm propelling while the left arm is extended forward and kept still — breathing taking place to the right. This should be practised to the opposite side. Another helpful variation is to swim a mixture of front and back crawl, rolling on every third arm pull. The swimmer should be encouraged to swim widths or lengths at both slow and fast speeds.

Breast stroke

The prerequisites for this stroke are as follows.

1. The ability to float prone for at least 6 seconds in the following positions:

(a) prone float with the arms extended, the hands touching with the palms facing downwards; the head should be in the water between the arms; the knees are bent so that the heels are close to the hips and the feet everted;
(b) prone float as above but the legs are extended and abducted with the feet everted;
(c) prone float as above but the legs are extended and adducted and the feet are pointed backwards.

The body must remain flat and any rolling action caused by body asymmetry corrected if possible.

The swimmer progresses the prone float by slowly changing the body shape, moving through the three stages (a), (b) and (c) above. This results in a symmetrical leg action for breast stroke. This should be practised until the movements are habitual, and the arm actions are not introduced until this is attained.

2. The swimmer should be able to jump forwards unaided.

3. The swimmer should be able to dive through an arch provided by two therapists or through the therapist's legs. This latter skill simulates the arm action of breast stroke as the swimmer passes through the arch of the therapist's legs. Once submerged, the hands are parted to hold the therapist's on either side or, in the case of going through the legs, the calves of the therapist, against which the swimmer now pulls and then pushes to pass through the arch. The breast stroke leg action is not employed when passing under the arch because it may result in someone being kicked. If a leg action is required, that of the front crawl stroke may be used.

The co-ordination of the arm and leg actions is most quickly achieved with the swimmer submerged. A long arm pull with the hands finishing at the thighs is encouraged. When performing breast stroke at the surface, the chin should be kept at the surface and the arm pull should become smaller, the hands never passing beyond the shoulder, and the action of the limbs should be within the body line. The pattern of movement for a continuous stroke is 'pull, kick', 'pull, kick', but for a more leisurely stroke the pattern of movement is 'pull, kick, glide'. Where co-ordination is not maintained, an examination of the action of the limbs is necessary. The fault usually lies with an imbalance in the reciprocal action of arms and legs, one pair of limbs having a larger action than the other. Accordingly, modification of either the kicking or pulling action is needed.

The co-ordination of breathing can be performed in two ways. The first is carried out in shallow water, the swimmer adopting a prone float with the head raised to allow the arms to be extended forwards parallel with the surface of the water. The head is raised enough to allow the feet to sink. The face remains submerged at eyebrow level and the feet drag on the floor of the pool. While floating in this position, the arms are pressed backwards and slightly downwards on the water. Such action will cause the face to clear the surface of the water automatically. The swimmer is instructed to exhale while the face is submerged, inhalation occurring as a reflex action as the face clears the surface. Breast stroke swimming can take place with the face immersed, the eyes looking forwards and the breathing co-ordinated with the arm action as indicated.

The second approach to breathing co-ordination is through a combination of head-up breast stroke and also swimming submerged. One complete stroke with the face immersed is followed by one with the head up. This results in breast stroke with alternate breathing — that is, breathing on every other stroke. From this the swimmer should proceed to breathing on every stroke.

Techniques and modification of strokes

Techniques and modifications of strokes for specific conditions have been dealt with in the section concerned with disability. However, many of the progressions already cited lend themselves well to the teaching of strokes in particular disabilities. For instance, when instructing a swimmer who is only able to use one arm, the progression for front crawl stroke — where side floating, breathing and one arm action are involved — would prove effective. Adaptations of strokes have been advocated by other authors (Elkington, 1978; Price, 1980) along with the use of flotation equipment. The author discourages the use of such equipment for a number of reasons.

First, marked alterations in shape and density make it extremely difficult for the therapist to know precisely where the flotation equipment should be placed on the body or limbs. The swimmer will undoubtedly alter the body shape while working in the water, and this tends to nullify the value of the flotation apparatus and causes the swimmer to become unbalanced.

Second, swimmers who become dependent on flotation equipment may resist its removal. Therefore, they are distinguished always from their able-bodied or less dependent peers by the flotation equipment, which must always be securely attached to them. They thus fail to achieve the aim of independence in water.

Third, with the exception of some makes of life-saving jackets, no flotation equipment offers complete safety in all circumstances. The vigilance of the care-giver is still required constantly, and if this is so, the swimmer would be better served by learning to cope with the balance and rotational problems of the body without the false sense of security engendered by aids.

Finally, the disabled are living in a world made special by virtue of the disability and its needs. Many of these needs involve the use of aids and appliances to assist movement. In water, movement becomes easier and is more readily obtained, and total independence can be achieved. The disabled person discards the aids and appliances used on land and is able to enjoy the freedom of movement water provides. Why then are aids and appliances advocated for water? Surely this is denying the joys and delight of such freedom of movement and independence.

Many of the ideas provided in the section on dynamic activities form part of the build-up to swimming and independent movement and furnish the swimmer with activities that supplement those of strokes. They all demand propulsion, and thereby competence in that area is attained. Additionally, changes of shape, speed and direction are required and this provides extra awareness of body image and of the body in space.

The swimming programme should be made as varied and interesting as possible and the potential of any swimmer developed to the level the swimmer desires. This may include swimming for recreation, fitness, competition, synchronised swimming, or may provide for participation in other aquatic sports.

The aim for all disabled must be that they swim in safety. However, for some disabled persons this will not be achieved, and activity in water for them must always be supervised.

RE-EDUCATION OF WALKING

The re-education of functional activities, especially walking, is a considerable part of activity in water.

The attainment and maintenance of the upright position and the balance and co-ordination required have been described. Activities for the acquisition of vertical rotation are numerous, and the judicious placing of turbulence (see p. 179) helps the person stabilise the body. A forward head and arm action ensures the feet remain on the floor of the pool, and this position should be adopted when commencing retraining the gait. If support from the therapist is necessary, then this should be provided from in front, using the facing hold (pp. 52, 53). Later, support is given from behind and gradually total disengagement is achieved.

The correct depth of water should be used — that is, the water should just cover the shoulders and should not be lower than the axillae. This provides a buoyancy-dominated situation and support to the whole body. As walking skills improve, the person may gradually be taken into shallower water, walking forwards, backwards and sideways from a buoyancy-dominated to a gravity-dominated environment. Transference of weight sideways should commence the re-education of walking. The feet are placed apart sideways as widely as necessary and the body weight moved over first one leg and then the other. Walking sideways can be carried out on a one-to-one basis, the person and therapist working together, or in a group using a circle formation.

Weight transference is progressed in the step standing position and support may be provided in the same sequence, moving from a buoyancy- to a gravity-dominated situation. Walking forwards is developed from the forwards and backwards 'rocking' action. It should be remembered that different muscle work is involved in walking in the water from that of walking on land (Duffield, 1976) as buoyancy assists and resists the movements of the lower limbs. For example, buoyancy assists hip and knee flexion but resists the lowering of the leg. Throughout gait retraining, the person will need to lean forward against the build-up of pressure in front of the body. However, when walking backwards the head and arms should still be kept forwards, for if the head is taken back, a loss of balance in the upright position will occur.

Balance and co-ordination can be further improved during gait retraining by instructing the person to pause and stabilise the body, not letting it be disturbed by turbulent effect created by the movement. If walking is performed in this way, the starting position is standing on one leg with the arms stretched forwards just below the surface of the water, with one leg raised in flexion at the hip, the knee extended and the foot dorsiflexed. The supporting knee should be extended. A step is taken onto the forward leg and the original supporting limb is allowed to extend at the hip, the pelvis remaining facing forwards, so that rotation of the pelvis and trunk does not take place. The steps taken may be very small at first, but can be increased gradually. If the person has difficulty in maintaining balance, the arms may be taken slowly sideways into abduction, thus bringing the centre of gravity back within the body. Once a stable position is achieved, the arms are moved forward in a controlled manner and the next part of the pattern commenced. The extended leg is brought forward with a straight knee and is raised forwards as high as possible. Buoyancy assists the flexion at the hip. The body is stabilised again before the next step is taken.

This 'goose-step' demands considerable control throughout the body, particularly as the size of the stride taken increases, producing greater turbulence. Eventually the person may jump onto one leg, pause to stabilise the body, before continuing the pattern. Again, deeper water is used at first, progressing to shallower water as control is gained. This method of gait retraining has, in the author's experience, proved valuable in both orthopaedic and neurological conditions. The person who has hemiplegia and whose gait deteriorates from time to time has benefited from a period of hydrotherapy using this technique. The pattern is not easily acquired, and careful instruction is necessary, but the majority of persons treated enjoy both the mental and physical exercise required in the acquisition of the skill. For the orthopaedic conditions this method can usually be progressed more rapidly. In one instance this gait retraining and other techniques developed on similar lines were of particular value in the rehabilitation of a ballet dancer who had suffered severe damage to one knee requiring surgery and prolonged rehabilitation. Progress was excellent and she finally returned to dancing on points with the ballet company.

PROGRAMMES

Planning programmes, setting objectives, implementing objectives and selection of activities

Programmes for groups and for individuals must be carefully planned in order that progress in activity in water proceeds for each child.

All skills should be acquired steadily and accurately so that ultimately each can be performed automatically. In this way the safety of each child can be assured. Some severely disabled will not achieve the final goal of being a mentally adjusted and physically balanced swimmer, safe under all conditions, but every effort should be made to ensure that the skills are developed in such a way as to minimise any weakness in ability.

The changes in shape and density of each child are variables to be considered both when planning the programme of activity and defining the specific objectives of exercise in water. For instance, a child suffering from juvenile chronic arthritis may have some flexion at the hips giving a triangular shape. This alteration of shape requires that in the initial stages the child should work in the vertical and supine lying positions. The specific objectives of exercise in water would be the reduction of pain and muscle spasm, the maintenance and increase of range of movement of joints, the strengthening of weak muscles, and improvement in mental and physical adaptability.

The organisation of the water activity programme should then include the objectives for each child, an outline of work and a table of required achievements. All of this should be recorded, together with details of each pool session, the water temperature, the duration of water activity and the activities employed. Details of progress must be recorded and should be checked at regular intervals. Progress can be achieved by playing the selected therapeutic game at an advanced level, or by choosing another game not previously played which demands the same skill. Similarly, specific objectives such as joint range and muscle power must be measured and recorded.

SURVIVAL SKILLS

Some disabled children can and do achieve advanced survival skills and take tests and awards in this aspect of water activity. Others, more severely disabled either physically or mentally, or both, may require such skills to be instilled for safety. In these circumstances survival skills should be taught by an experienced instructor and with the full knowledge of all concerned with the child.

The transition from swimming a few strokes under water and having to stand erect to take a breath, to swimming on the surface and therefore being able to participate more fully in any part of the pool and in any activity, was achieved for one Downs' syndrome child by jumping into deep water with a trusted and experienced instructor. When unable to stand up to take a breath, the child was disturbed, but, after repeating the jump five more times, was swimming on the surface, the old habit broken, and able to participate in an increased number of advanced activities, including racing.

AWARDS AND COMPETITIONS

A number of awards have been specifically designed for handicapped swimmers and provide goals for the children to attain. If at all possible, any child desirous of entering for awards should aim for those designed for able-bodied children, since this will prevent feelings of isolation and being different. Whatever type of award is undertaken, the child should understand that only a correct performance is acceptable.

Competitions should be entered with similar motives, and the method of racing advocated is by timed handicapping, as used in the Halliwick Method and by the Association of Swimming Therapy. This system allows all disabled to participate, needs no assessment other than of a swimmer's performance over a given distance, provides an incentive for each person to improve performance, and makes possible integrated competition for all disabled and able-bodied persons.

Chapter 3

SPECIFIC DISORDERS AND THEIR HANDLING

OSTEOGENESIS IMPERFECTA

Although osteogenesis imperfecta is a rare disease, it is one that can ideally receive physical treatment in water.

In the severe congenital form, frequent fractures are caused by minor trauma and the prognosis is poor. In the milder form the future is less bleak. For all the children, movement in water is easier than on land and there is less danger of fractures. Following surgery, especially of the long bones to correct deformity, weight-bearing in water in the upright position can be gradually introduced, provided the child is handled appropriately.

Great care must be taken when introducing the children to water, and it is preferable that severe cases are treated individually. The child with a milder form may benefit from group activity, but the therapist must guard against the child coming into sharp contact with other persons in the group or with the sides of the pool. It is advisable that the child does not jump into the water, nor land heavily on the feet, and diving is best avoided — although the author has worked with two children who had a very mild form of osteogenesis imperfecta and who eventually engaged in all such activities.

Growth is retarded and all the children will be small in stature, but not all are confined to wheelchairs, though this may be so in adult life.

Osteogenesis imperfecta congenita

This severe form may be seen in children's hospitals, and physical treatment may be requested both preoperatively and postoperatively.

Entry into the water can be effected in several ways but is best achieved with the child lying supine on a stretcher. In the case of the very young, small child, a tray made of suitable splinting material with sides and canvas handles may prove invaluable (Fig. 39). The child can remain on this throughout the treatment. The therapist supports the tray and can angle it so that the buoyancy of the water floats the limbs to be exercised off the tray, thus allowing free movement.

The child is invariably terrified at entering water, and it takes a long time, many pool sessions and much patience, to overcome the very real fears. The same situation will recur following surgical

Fig. 39 *Tray used for treatment of child with osteogenesis imperfecta congenita.*

Fig. 40 *First facing hold.*

treatment, even though the child is aware that the warmth of the water is comforting and movement easier.

Shape and density are important, particularly where deformities are marked, but until the child is actively exercising off the tray they are of lesser concern to the therapist.

Post-surgical treatment usually involves obtaining the upright position with the gradual introduction of weight-bearing in standing and walking. In addition, general mobilising and strengthening exercises for the limbs are introduced. Water depth is critical. The child should be taken to a sufficient depth so that in the vertical position the feet are initially clear of the floor of the pool. As weight-bearing is gradually permitted, the child is taken into less deep water. To ensure that the progression into shallower water is carefully graded, it is essential to record the exact depth at each treatment. Close co-operation with the surgeon in charge of the case in relation to the progression of weight-bearing is important.

The child will need to be made aware of how important head control is in maintaining the upright position. If the head is kept forward, the feet will remain down. The therapist should sit in a stable position supporting the child at the waist from in front. The child's arms should be forward and just under the surface, or resting on the therapist's arms (Fig. 40).

Cervical flexion and extension begun in a very

small range are then encouraged. The movement in each direction should be slow so that the child can appreciate the swing of the body and counteract the movement with the head.

Gentle, active movement of the legs is encouraged in this position — flexion/extension, abduction/adduction of the hips with the knees straight, and hip and knee flexion. These movements can also be performed in supine lying when the child is supported by the therapist's hands lightly held under the waist, with the child's head resting gently on the therapist's shoulders. The therapist must be in a stable sitting position with the shoulders under the water. In both positions active arm movements can be encouraged. From supine lying, forward recovery will not only encourage flexion and extension but also stress head control.

As further weight-bearing is allowed, activity is carried out in progressively shallow water. Weight transference should be encouraged from side to side — 'tick, tock' as the pendulum of a clock. This activity may be introduced before weight-bearing is permitted, and will develop lateral flexion of head and trunk. As with all activities, it is commenced in a small range at first. Step-standing weight transference is introduced next and then walking small steps, gradually extending the length of the stride. The walking pattern can be varied, walking with hip and knee flexion or with the knees extended. The therapist will support the child at the waist from in front at the commencement of all progressions — that is, in each new depth — and will gradually disengage by removing the waist support and allowing the child to hold on to the therapist's outstretched arms, working towards a hand hold, fingertip hold and total independence.

While working in front of the child, the therapist has good eye contact and communication is easy. For progression and further disengagement, the therapist walks behind the child with arms stretched forward so that the child's hands or arms can rest on them.

All movements should be slow and rhythmical. Any sudden movement may cause trauma and must be avoided. These children therefore require a one-to-one basis for hydrotherapy. If other help is available, it can be very useful. However, it depends on the nature of the child–parent relationship and attitude as to whether parents are used in this assistant role. In the author's experience, the parents' help should be at the bathside, in dressing and undressing, lifting and handling into and out of the pool — daily activities they are used to performing.

Milder forms of osteogenesis imperfecta can be treated on similar lines to those of other orthopaedic conditions. However, the treatment sessions should be handled cautiously and progressions made more gradually. The child progresses well towards swimming, and provided awareness of the precautions to be taken are instilled, this should present no difficulties. It is essential that rolling is taught, especially rolling on to the bar, so that when swimming back stroke and nearing the end of the pool, no sudden hard contact occurs with the walls of the pool. The ability to keep the eyes open when taking part in water activity is essential.

JUVENILE CHRONIC ARTHRITIS

This is the name by which juvenile rheumatoid arthritis is more commonly known today. There are inflammatory changes involving soft tissues in and around the joints and bones and articular cartilages. The joints most usually affected are those of the knees, hips, ankles, wrists, metacarpophalangeal and cervical spine. The condition may affect a single joint or many joints.

The onset of the condition usually occurs at an early age and thus most patients will undergo treatment for a prolonged period of time. These are the formative years when normal physical, intellectual, social and emotional development will be disrupted. For these reasons it is important that the child leads as normal a life as possible and that treatment is made a pleasurable time.

Joint range and function must be maintained, and programmes of active daily exercises are provided. Not only affected joints must be exercised, so activities should be used which offer the opportunity to achieve as full a range of movement as possible in all joints and allow the child to gain socially and emotionally as well.

Hydrotherapy provides these ideal conditions, particularly when therapeutic exercises can be hidden in a programme of games and activities that are fun and which lead on to swimming — a sport which the child will be able to use throughout life and which provides social contacts.

The warmth of the water provides relief of pain and muscle spasm, and buoyancy relieves the strain on joints, particularly the weight-bearing joints.

The aims of hydrotherapy are to:

(a) relieve pain,
(b) aid relaxation,
(c) increase range of movement and muscle strength,
(d) decrease deformity,
(e) improve functional ability.

The children may be referred for hydrotherapy while still on bed rest as they are able to exercise in a non-weight-bearing situation and stand and walk partially weight-bearing. In the chronic stage, hydrotherapy is an excellent medium for rehabilitation.

The therapist must observe the child's shape and density. Alterations in the former will come about due to the pain, muscle spasm and joint changes. Density may be altered due to the loss of muscle bulk which can result from the decrease in use caused by pain. In practice, it is advisable to introduce the child to the water gently and quietly at first, observing all the points of handling and entry mentioned earlier in Chapter 2.

The young child in pain will be anxious about going into water and may exhibit fear. A one-to-one relationship within a group situation is desirable, but at first care should be taken to avoid joining a group that contains other extremely active children.

Games which attract the child's attention and divert the thoughts from the anxieties and pain should be introduced immediately following entry, and the therapist should be using activities in both a therapeutic and recreational manner. An awareness of which joints are most affected is important, and activities directed towards exercising them and strengthening the muscles surrounding them must be used. As with all children and all water activity, it is advantageous to encourage blowing on to and into the water from the earliest time. In addition to the effects on respiration, such action induces the forward movement of the head and encourages flexion of neck and trunk. The range of abduction and adduction of the hip joints may need to be increased and muscle power strengthened. If the child is non-weight-bearing due to pain in the hip joints, these can be exercised in supine lying supported by the therapist at the centre of balance of the body, with the head resting on the therapist's shoulder, when 'Twinkle, twinkle little star' could be used for the younger child and 'Stars and Stripes' for the older age group. However, if partial weight-bearing is possible, and as a progression, walking sideways using any of the circle games could be used. It is important that the child does not cross the legs, that a step is taken to the side and the other leg brought to it, otherwise the effect of overcoming turbulence and leaning against the water, together with the necessity of increasing the size of the steps, is lost. Circle games also have the advantage of making the child aware of the weight of water and that it can be leant against. Lateral head control is required, which means that some cervical side flexion and, incidentally, trunk side flexion occurs, particularly when the circle direction is changed and turbulence has to be overcome. Cervical flexion and extension and side flexion can be encouraged if the playing of 'Here we go round the mulberry bush' is extended to include verses such as 'This is the way we blow bubbles' (flexion), 'This is the way we nod our heads' (flexion and extension), 'This is the way we wash our ears' (side flexion), and 'This is the way we wash our hair' (extension with some rotation). Rotation is encouraged in all activities that include lateral rotation, either in the vertical or horizontal plane, for example 'Space ships', 'Looby Loo', 'The hokey cokey' or 'Passing the ring'.

Fingers, wrists, ankles, knees and hips can be exercised in the game 'If you're happy and you know it'. The child can make rain with the fingers and hands and good 'splashes' with the legs when lying supine, the emphasis being laid upon whichever joints require most attention. Saying 'hallo' and 'goodbye' to the toes and feet exercises the metatarso-phalangeal and ankle joints; taking the heels down and toes up to catch a fish and bring it to the surface encourages knee flexion and hip extension. Passing a light plastic beach ball held between the feet around a circle in the supine lying position increases muscle work and range of movement in all joints of the lower limbs. Ball games played with the upper limbs in the upright position do the same for these. Making waves with the arms unilaterally or bilaterally increases shoulder movement and muscle strength in addition to trunk rotation. The child should at first stretch the arms out in front and clasp the hands. Later, as a progression and to increase the muscle work, the child should hold the hands and arms shoulder width apart. For total flexion and extension of the body with shoulder movements involved, the teaching of vertical rotation in such activities as 'Catch an object' or 'Reaching for the bar' is excellent. Vertical rotation requires precise balance in the vertical position against turbulence, which improves balance and co-ordination. 'Bells', where the child uses flexion and extension of the cervical spine to swing the body in a 'ball' shape, can be extended to total flexion and extension in 'Rag dolls' and 'The wind, sun and rain'.

Bicycle riding is advocated as an interesting activity on land to maintain movements in the ankles and knees to encourage knee extension especially, and to improve and maintain muscle strength. 'Bicycles' in the water is great fun also; it is incorporated in many of the activities and can be used to teach vertical rotational control. A modified bicycle forearm hold is valuable where there are any changes in the shoulder and cervical joints causing pain. The child is supported by the therapist using the bicycle forearm hold, the modification being that the child is held close to the therapist, who uses a stable sitting position with legs widely spaced. Undue pressure on the shoulder, acromioclavicular and cervical spine joints is avoided in this modification of the hold. The child is held so that the feet are clear of the bottom of the pool, but must not be lifted too high out of the water as this will increase the downward effects of gravity on the child and prove tiring for the therapist. To increase range of movement in the hip joints, the child is asked to abduct the legs 'to let the boats go through' and adduct them 'to close the lock gates', keeping the knees extended. Combined hip and knee flexion, either alternately or together, can be likened to a 'lift going up and down'. If the scissor action of flexion and extension of the hips with straight knees is required, the child should be held to one side of the therapist, close to the body with the same arm hold.

An imaginative therapist can devise many ways in which to divert the child and provide a pleasurable means of exercise, at the same time familiarising the child with the element of water and leading the activities towards swimming.

For the child with juvenile chronic arthritis who may have involvement of the thoracic spine, breathing control is as essential as for any other child. The therapist should ensure not only that the skill of blowing on to, into and out under water becomes an automatic one, but that activities specifically designed for teaching breathing control are included in the programme.

Although specific swimming strokes are advocated by some writers, the children's degree of mobility should be the guiding factor in their selection. In the author's experience, the children frequently 'paddle' off in activities such as 'The big ship sails down the Alley, Alley O' using what mobility they have. They should be encouraged to improve stroking in the classic styles of crawl, back stroke and breast stroke, the last of which may be restricted by limited abduction of the legs. Side stroke can be used to advantage with some children.

MUSCULAR DYSTROPHY

There are a number of clinical descriptions of muscular dystrophy, a disease characterised by progressive degenerative processes in the skeletal muscles. That most commonly seen is the Duchenne-type muscular dystrophy. The activity in water described in this section is applicable not only to this type, but also to other diseases demonstrating muscle weakness, such as spinal muscular atrophy.

Duchenne-type muscular dystrophy is an inherited disorder usually seen in males. It is sex linked and transmitted by an unaffected female.

In the first four years of life the early signs become apparent. The child finds increasing difficulty in walking, enlargement of muscles occurs, together with muscle weakness which begins proximally in the pelvic and shoulder girdles and progresses until the child is unable to walk. Despite weakness in the shoulders and arms, some hand function is retained until a later stage.

The increasing muscle weakness in the flexors and extensors of the hip and the extensors of the knee, combined with that of the trunk and pelvic girdle, creates difficulties in maintaining the erect posture against gravity, with resultant hip and knee flexion, scoliotic and lordotic deformities.

Respiratory function is affected by the disease, more markedly if there is spinal deformity.

Due to the progressive muscle weakness, resultant deformity and changes in muscle tissue, shape and density will be considerably altered in these children. The alteration will be increasingly marked as the disease progresses, and the therapist will need to be alert to the changes when taking the child into the water.

The advantages of activity in water for these children are:

(a) water mobility is encouraged and can be maintained long after activity on land has become extremely difficult,

(b) stamina and endurance can be encouraged,

(c) respiratory function is enhanced,

(d) a social and recreational activity is established that can be enjoyed with others, enabling a happier and more interesting active life to be maintained.

The aim of activity in water should be to teach the child to swim. For this, mental adjustment, breathing and balance control must be developed. In the early stages of the disease while the child is still ambulant, these skills should be acquired as quickly as possible so that there is a long period of time in which the child can enjoy swimming and take part in other aquatic activities if desired.

By the choice of appropriate games, specific activities to maintain range of movement, the erect posture and walking can be incorporated in the child's programme. As the disease progresses these will have to be modified. Emphasis is placed by the therapist on the component of movement required at any point in the activity.

Effective stretchings are not easily carried out in water as it is difficult to acquire sufficient stability of either the child or the therapist. Modified movements of the Bad Ragaz Ring method (Davis, 1967; Boyle, 1981) can be introduced for early stretching of some joints, but in time the increasing muscle weakness renders the use of these techniques impractical. Where a scoliosis is presenting, it is possible to get some active contraction on the side of the convexity and stretching of the concave side by the use of the technique described on p. 207 under the heading of Hemiplegia.

Certain general points need to be considered.

1. The increasing muscle weakness.
2. The increasing deformities.
3. The involvement of the respiratory muscles and the risk of respiratory infections.
4. The child's personal attitude to the disease and the anxiety that develops with the progressive weakness.

Increasing muscle weakness

The child is less and less able to create movement in the water, particularly those movements of vertical and lateral rotation. Consequently the child is at greater risk and care must be taken to ensure safety. Facilitation of rolling and forward recovery eventually becomes necessary.

As muscle changes take place, so the density of the child alters and there will be a tendency for those parts which have become less dense to float higher. Floating is usually easy for the child but, for comfort, happiness and safety, floating should be in the supine position. In the later stages of the disease the child may have little strength to maintain the head at water level in the supine position, the nose and mouth being all of the face that is above water. If the child is anxious about this situation, some means of flotation for the head may be of value. Since flotation collars are often restrictive, a large swimming cap, inside and at the back of which a plastic bag filled with the required number of polystyrene balls can be appropriately placed may be useful.

Increasing deformities

The increasing deformities will alter the shape of the child, and adjustments to body position, balance and rotational control will need to be made. The alterations in shape will occur slowly and the therapist should be constantly alert for them. While specific work to maintain a reasonable range of movement and prevent deformity may be possible in the early stages, as the disease progresses it is unrealistic to continue stretchings or other specific exercises. Walking in water can be continued after it has ceased to be possible on land, even if it is achieved only by rotation of the shoulders in the vertical. Support will gradually be required and should be given by the therapist from in front as in the facing hold (see Fig. 19), especially as the ability to control the head decreases and the child's fear of losing balance in the vertical grows.

Involvement of respiratory function

The involvement of the muscles of respiration makes inspiration and expiration increasingly ineffective. In the early stages, 'blowing' and encouraging the good breathing control required for swimming will aid respiratory function. It will be necessary to ensure, at all times, that the child is not exposed to extra risk of infection through activity in water. Changing areas should be free from draughts and appropriately heated, and adequate drying of the body and hair is essential. The child should not participate if feeling unwell, since this suggests an infection could be present.

The child's attitude to the disease

The child with muscular dystrophy needs constant encouragement. The condition will place a growing number of restrictions on the ability to achieve, however hard the child tries. The continual failure causes depression, and negative attitudes develop. Water is one environment in which movement and enjoyment can be maintained for longer. However, the child does become aware of the ability to move less and less well in the water. With the loss of control due to muscle weakness, there is the fear of losing balance and of being unable to recover to a safe breathing position. This affects the attitude to water activity. The therapist will need to encourage the child but must avoid activities which are too difficult. More and more manual support has to be given and should be at the centre of balance of the body whatever the hold. The exception is for the vertical position in the later stages when the 'floppy hold' (see Fig. 21a and b) may be used. At all times, the emphasis should be on independence, but the child must not be faced with frequent failure.

SPINA BIFIDA

Spina bifida refers to a congenital abnormality in which there is a failure of closure in the midline of neural, bony or soft tissue (Carmel, 1974). It is among the commonest major congenital abnormalities and is often associated with others such as hydrocephalus, congenitally dislocated hips, and talipes equino varus.

Spina bifida is usually classified as being of two main types:

(a) spina bifida occulta,
(b) spina bifida cystica,

and under the last heading meningocele and myelomeningocele are described.

It is the child with myelomeningocele who most concerns the physiotherapist (Shepherd, 1980). Such cases would be the ones more frequently treated in water, since the milder forms of spina bifida rarely present problems, and activity in water for this group would almost certainly follow that for the able-bodied.

The child with a myelomeningocele will have marked alterations in both shape and density, and this will be a major consideration when undertaking activity in water. Other considerations relate to hydrocephalus, if present, incontinence, lack of sensation, social and psychological factors.

The need to study the shape and density of the spina bifida child in relation to activity in water cannot be too strongly emphasised. As a background to this, the hydrodynamic principles, characteristics and properties of water and all aspects of rotation must be fully understood.

Alterations in shape and density in spina bifida

These vary considerably with each individual child, but the common and frequent complications are:

(a) the loss of density in the lower limbs leading to high floating of these limbs,
(b) the ease with which vertical balance can be disturbed or lost,
(c) the rotational problems occurring due to asymmetric distribution of muscle power and deformity.

The child affected by spina bifida must learn the effect of head movement on the body, particularly anteriorly and posteriorly, and thereby appreciate how the head controls the body position and the feet. Any action that takes the head back and away, or forward and away, from the vertical will cause a quick upswing of the legs and trunk with rotation. This loss of balance is a disturbing experience and usually causes the child to cling to the therapist, the bar or the side of the pool in an effort to maintain the vertical position.

In the early stages, control of vertical rotation must therefore be strongly emphasised until it becomes an automatic response. Instruction should begin in the 'ball' shape and at first only small rocking movements should be permitted. These movements can be widened as control is gained. 'Bells' provides an excellent means of teaching such control and should be done on a one-to-one basis, progressing to less support with a short arm hold between two therapists and eventually to a 'Rag dolls' swinging action.

The 'bicycling' action and hold employed in a number of activities, such as 'Bicycles', 'Looby Loo' and 'The wheels of the bus', encourage a fine degree of vertical rotation control, and when this has been gained progress can be pursued through activities which involve the extremes of posture from 'ball' to 'stick', such as in 'Eggs for breakfast'.

Vertical or forward recovery requires a quick movement, since a 'sinking' action is required if the legs are to go down and the upright position be obtained. To create forward recovery, the knees must be flexed towards the chin as much as possible, the head and arms stretched forward to rotate the body from supine lying to the vertical. To facilitate the forward head movement and to encourage breathing control, the swimmer should blow out as the head is brought forward. Where high-floating legs make the 'sinking' action difficult, the arms may be carried up above the water, thus increasing the gravitational effect and, therefore, the 'sinking' action. Since the paralysis may not be equally distributed in both legs, there will be a tendency for one leg to float higher than the other. In this instance the arms need to be taken above the water surface and carried to the side on which the higher floating leg is. This causes rotation over that side and enables the swimmer to regain the vertical position. Balance is then maintained by appropriate head control and the forward position of the arms.

'Rag dolls' and other activities designed to encourage the swimmer to move from the supine to the prone position in the water are a natural progression as the degree of head control is developed and lessens anxiety. Such progression has to be steadily but surely developed as the child will have considerable anxiety about the changes of body position anteriorly and posteriorly.

Encouragement of the supine lying position from the vertical is the first progression, and when such control has been achieved, moving to prone from the vertical is next, then progressing to swinging actions between supine and prone.

When vertical rotational control is achieved, the

child will be more mentally adjusted to water and physical balance will be better controlled. However, problems of lateral rotation may have to be considered and this control should be taught along with vertical rotational control. The need for consideration of lateral rotational control will have been evident when observing the asymmetry of the child's body along the longitudinal axis in supine. All rotational alterations, however small, will be seen and the importance of teaching lateral rotational control obvious. Such control is taught in the vertical, half lying, and finally in the horizontal positions. The child learns to control any longitudinal rotational effects by turning the head away from the side rolling under the water. Activities which teach lateral rotation firstly in the vertical plane and through to the horizontal plane should be developed. Examples of such activities in the vertical are 'turning' and 'Jumping on the spot' and they also form part of activities such as 'Looby Loo' or 'The hokey cokey', 'Space ships' and 'Passing an object around the circle'. Games such as 'Seaweed', 'Hallo' and 'Rolling on to the bar' assist in the progression towards horizontal lateral rotation. Complete rolling through 360° follows with the therapist 'patting' the body around to facilitate the roll until the swimmer is able to produce the roll to either side independently, blowing as the face goes towards and is submerged in the water.

When vertical and lateral rotation have been achieved and the swimmer can roll horizontally in both directions and recover forward from lying to a safe breathing position, it is necessary to combine both rotations for final control prior to underwater activity and 'paddling off'.

The author is convinced that it is the disturbing effect of loss of balance that causes much anxiety in the spina bifida child. This is most evident in the prone position which produces marked degrees of trunk and cervical extension. This troubles the child excessively and it appears that activities carried out in the vertical and supine positions are best adhered to at first until a considerable degree of vertical rotation control has been acquired. Lateral rotation should be introduced and then a combination of both rotations until the child progressively develops skills which lead to complete mental adaptability and balance control.

Due to the frequency of losing balance in the backward or, more frequently, forward direction, the child is often forced into the prone position. To counteract this the head is usually extended strongly, and encouraging the child to get the head forward and blow into the water is difficult.

If the size of the child's head is increased, it will mean that the centre of buoyancy will be higher in the body than in children not suffering from this problem. This will compound the difficulty of vertical rotational control, as even the slightest movement of the head forwards or backwards will increase to a marked degree the loss of balance and quick upswing of the legs in either direction.

These two points emphasise the importance of teaching vertical rotational control.

Children who have hydrocephalus associated with spina bifida will almost invariably have had surgery with the insertion of a shunt or valve to control the condition. Care must be taken not to press on the valve, which will be *in situ* behind the ear. Heads should not be held (see p. 9), but in these children there is the added problem of the shunt. The abnormal head size, even in those children whose hydrocephalus has been arrested, makes the development of head control an onerous task. Balance is slow to develop and will need attention, but all activities in water have, inherently, a balance component.

Due to difficulties in maintaining the vertical position, the spina bifida child has a great need to cling either to the therapist or the bar, and disengagement is another step in progress that needs strong emphasis.

Activities that encourage such disengagement are 'How wide? How tall?', 'Hickory, dickory, dock', 'Looby Loo', 'Space ships', 'walking' round the circle and all those other activities which have the child facing away from the therapist, such as 'Eggs for breakfast', 'Bicycles' and 'Space ships'.

Swimming becomes a reality for the child only when it has acquired all rotational control, is able to disengage and appreciates upthrust.

Therapeutically the child will have acquired much activity for head, trunk, legs and arms, and through independent mobility will have worked those muscles which have some power.

Entry and exit

The child with spina bifida and/or hydrocephalus can enter over the side (see p. 44). The problem in entry is the fear of loss of balance and lack of trunk control as the hands are placed on the therapist's shoulders. This may be overcome by secure handling, verbal reassurance, frequent repetition of the mode of entry, and, for entry to the water, the choice of a rhyme or song that appeals to the child.

The form of exit from the pool can be over the side, but if the child has had a urinary diversion which involves the wearing of a bag attached to a stoma, the hip on the side of the stoma must be lifted well clear of the side of the pool as progress from the water and 'wriggling' along the poolside take place. Thus the bag is not disturbed (Fig. 41).

Incontinence

Children with myelomeningocele will have bowel and bladder incontinence. The former is usually managed by appropriate diet and training and, if managed well, is not a problem during activity in water, though it should be ascertained that the bowels have been evacuated that day (Trussell,

Fig. 41a *'Normal' exit over the side.*

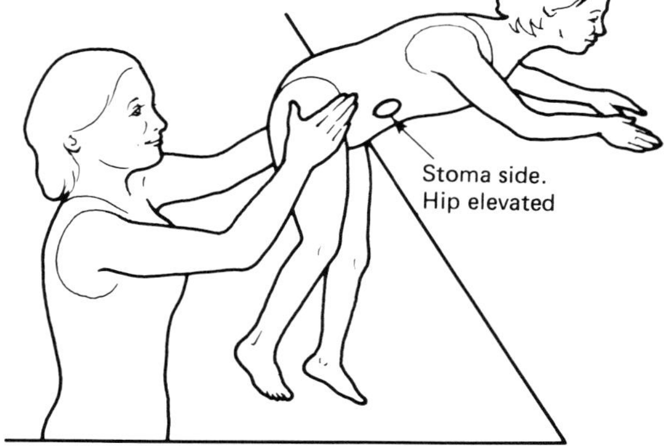

Fig. 41b *Modification of exit over the side for spina bifida child with stoma and bag.*

1971; Skinner and Thomson, 1983). Bladder incontinence presents a different problem, but does not act as a total contraindication provided suitable precautions are taken.

If the spina bifida child is being trained by expression of urine, this must be attended to prior to entering the water. If a bag of any type is worn, it should be emptied before the child enters the water and the tap secured in a closed position.

The wearing of plastic pants under the swimwear, especially those fastening at the side with press studs, is an added precaution. Plastic pants with elasticated openings may prove tight and uncomfortable and cause pressure on skin that has no sensation and poor nutrition, and should only be used provided such problems do not arise.

If at any particular time the spina bifida child appears to be, or is confirmed to be, 'off colour', water activity should be avoided until the child is well again as an infection may be developing.

Social and psychological factors

Social and psychological factors may be associated with the problems of incontinence. This presents a difficulty only where such children swim in public facilities. Appropriate and tactful handling can minimise these factors.

For the spina bifida child, learning to swim — which many ultimately do extremely well — offers the same beneficial social and psychological effects as in any other condition.

CEREBRAL PALSY

Cerebral palsy is one of the more common handicapping conditions, varying a great deal in degree of severity, distribution and in its effect on intellectual ability.

'The cerebral defect commonly results in disorders of movement and tone referred to as spasticity, rigidity, flaccidity, athetosis and ataxia' (Shepherd, 1980), and these are frequently accompanied by associated disorders of vision and hearing, intellectual retardation and perceptual problems. All these will have a bearing on the child's activity in water and must be taken into account when working in the water with such a child.

It is beyond the scope of this book to discuss in detail the aetiology and characteristics of types of cerebral palsy, but categorising the children according to the distribution of the motor involvement is helpful when considering taking them into water. The distributions most commonly met with are hemiplegia, diplegia and quadriplegia. The alterations in body shape and density that occur as a result of the motor involvement need to be studied carefully and the programme for each child developed accordingly.

The major problems which will confront the therapist when taking cerebral palsied children into water are:

(a) altered shape and density,
(b) an inability to create voluntary movement readily due to spasticity,
(c) an inability to control the involuntary movement of athetosis and ataxia,
(d) poor respiration,
(e) difficulties with comprehension and communication.

The problem can be further compounded by perceptual disorders, difficulties with head control, poor postural tone and lack of rotation within the body axis.

The problems will be discussed under the major categories of distribution.

The hemiplegic child

The hemiplegic child will have altered shape and possibly altered density, though the latter may only be slight or more evident in older children. Asymmetry of posture is noticeable in both the young child and older child, and a pattern that involves flexion and abduction of the leg is found, while the arm tends to be retracted, flexed and abducted. Alternatively, the arm may show signs of extension when the head is turned towards the affected side due to the influence of the asymmetrical tonic neck reflex. Most hemiplegic children dislike the prone position because the affected arm remains flexed and is often caught under the child's chest.

This can also occur if the child is placed prone in the water. It is then impossible to bring the arm forward and reach out. There may be difficulty in extending the head to keep the face clear of the water, and to achieve this the child may turn the head to one side. If the influence of the asymmetrical tonic neck reflex is strong, arm movements may be further inhibited. Add to this an overall anxiety about being in water and it will readily be seen that these children should be kept in the vertical position for their early activities, progressing later to supine lying.

The alteration in shape with 'shortening' of the affected side can be described as having the form of an unequal quadrilateral. The child will then tend to roll to the affected side (see Fig. 5b).

Correction of this rotation can be obtained by encouraging the child to rotate the head away from the affected side, whether in the vertical or horizontal supine position. The movement of the head will help to bring the body flat, thus developing a balanced position. The rotation of the head should be limited to that required to bring the body to a flat position. The head should not be allowed to turn so far as to affect the limbs if the asymmetrical tonic neck reflex is present.

In trying to equalise the unequal quadrilateral shape of the child, activities that involve lateral rotation in the vertical and horizontal planes are valuable. These activities include 'Looby Loo' and 'Space ships' where lateral rotation in the upright position is one pattern of movement in the total activity. Games such as 'Seaweed, 'Resisted rolling' and 'Rolling on to the bar' encourage lateral rotation in the horizontal plane.

A useful activity to increase symmetry is manual rolling to the affected side. The therapist supports the child, who is in supine, by placing the upturned hands just below the child's waist. The child is requested to turn the face to the side opposite to which the body is being rolled. The therapist then resists this induced counter-rotation so the child must work harder to restore the flat position, and extension occurs on the affected side.

Once improved symmetry is obtained, other skills will be acquired more easily. If the child is markedly 'shorter' on the affected side and the roll cannot be corrected solely by a turn of the head in the supine position, then the affected leg may be crossed over the unaffected leg, either at the ankle or knee, depending on the amount of roll that requires correcting. The nearer to the centre of balance of the body the limbs are crossed, the greater the effect. If the turning of the head and crossing of the legs are not sufficient to counter the roll to the affected side, the affected arm can be taken across the body when the additional weight will assist in controlling the higher-floating unaffected side. Once the body has found a balanced position, activities that will encourage a more equal shape should be emphasised.

The hemiplegic child may tend to swim in circles

at first. This is largely due to an inability to equalise arm movements but may also be the result of an asymmetry of shape.

When acquiring swimming strokes, therefore, the hemiplegic must learn to move the limbs in as equal a range as possible, gradually extending the range. If the child starts swimming on the back, arm movements should be equal and bilateral and the arms should initially be kept in the water. The back crawl leg action should be modified so that each leg acts equally. There is a tendency for a total flexion pattern of the affected leg to occur, the knee coming too far out of the water, and meta-centric effects result, with rotation of the body to the affected side with each kick.

Another way in which a flat position for swimming may be achieved in supine is by the child using the unaffected arm in an extended position underneath that side. By creating turbulence beneath the unaffected and potentially higher-floating side, the child can independently roll the body flat. The affected arm is used in a paddling action at the side of the swimmer.

If the child swims in the prone position, 'dog paddle' is probably the easiest stroke to commence with. This can be gradually progressed to breast stroke, again ensuring limb movements of the affected and unaffected sides are kept equal in range.

Side stroke is frequently useful. However, it is essential that the child has the affected side lowest in the water and that both arms and both legs are involved in the action. All too frequently one sees the hemiplegic swimming side stroke with the affected side uppermost, the limbs of that side moving into abnormal patterns as the unaffected side makes increasing efforts to propel the child through the water.

Although time and patience are required, it is not only desirable but possible to achieve swimming in a straight line. As the strokes used become more proficient, competitive swimming can be undertaken should the child so wish.

The affected arm and hand require particular attention if these outcomes are to be achieved. Additionally, it is essential that the upper limb — more likely to be neglected by the child — should be stimulated.

Already it has been appreciated that vertical balance in water requires that the head and arms should be kept forward. This must constantly be encouraged in the hemiplegic in walking, jumping and hopping. Activities which have as their teaching point vertical rotation not only develop patterns of total flexion and extension and precise balance, but can encourage bilateral arm action if a bar is reached for, toes caught, larger objects retrieved or, in 'Eggs for breakfast', the child has an 'egg' for each hand.

In any activity which requires a bicycle hold, symmetry and awareness of the affected arm can be enhanced by the use of a 'handle bar' or 'steering wheel'. A 1-foot long (30 cm), 1-inch diameter (2.5 cm) stick, either wood or electric wiring conduit, makes a useful handle bar and a quoit, 9–12 inches (23–30 cm) in diameter, a good steering wheel. The 'stick' provides a pronated grasp and the hoop a grasp in mid position between supination and pronation.

This equipment can also be used in activities such as 'Seaweed', 'Hallo' and 'Speedboats', when the child should be encouraged to aid symmetry by holding it as low on the body as possible with both hands while being swayed through the water, or towed while kicking the legs.

Awareness of the affected limbs, especially the arm, can be obtained in activities that require large movements. Making waves, splashing with the hands and kicking require balance control whether performed in the vertical or horizontal position. At first the therapist will need to assist with balance control, holding at the child's waist from behind, gradually reducing the amount of support as the child gains such control.

Since the hemiplegic child has a tendency to contract the trunk on the affected side, trunk and postural work are important. Resisted rolling (see p. 142) is valuable to produce contraction of the trunk extensors and side flexors of the unaffected side.

The therapist can also hold the child in supine lying by standing with the child's legs abducted either side of her waist, supporting along the lateral border of the thighs and pelvis with the forearms and hands. Swaying the child gently from side to side gradually induces relaxation. The speed of the swaying has to be adjusted to each individual's needs. Too fast a swing may produce an inappropriate response. Water going onto the face may also cause such a response. In this position both trunk flexion and limb flexion with rotation can be employed. The child is asked to sit up towards the therapist, the arms reaching towards the therapist's shoulders. To introduce rotation the child brings the body and arms forward towards the opposite shoulder of the therapist. In lying back the child must control the head and body action. It is important that the therapist bends her knees and 'goes down' as the child comes forward, rising again as the child lies back.

In order to work the trunk side flexors on the unaffected side, the child is held in the same position, but the body is swayed to the unaffected side and the child instructed to bend to that side when sufficient turbulent or drag effect has been created. To return to the starting position, a gentle passive swing without side flexion is used.

The diplegic child

The child who has spastic diplegia has altered shape: this will be triangular due mainly to the pattern of flexion at hip and knees (see p. 22). Since water floats triangular shapes point downwards, these children should begin water activity in the vertical and supine positions and not be placed prone at first, as in the prone position they will have to contend with this effect of the water. Additionally, the child may not have sufficient cervical and trunk extension to lift the face clear of the water to breathe, thus causing anxiety, tension and a further alteration in shape.

The diplegic child finds it difficult or impossible to balance in the upright position due to a narrow standing or walking base. In water, where stability and balance are at first less easily obtained, and the establishment of a wide base for stability is important, the diplegic child faces considerable problems. Abduction is difficult and it is therefore not possible to walk sideways. So activities which will gradually enable the child to change the shape, control balance and stabilise the body position must be part of the programme.

The distribution of the diplegic's spasticity is rarely symmetrical, so the additional problem of rotation to the more affected side is present. As with the hemiplegic child, rotation of the head away from the side rolling under the water will counter this effect.

To alter shape in the diplegic child, extension of the lower limbs should be encouraged along with abduction. Activities in the vertical position which are helpful are the circle games in which not only is the child made aware that water has weight, but, in walking sideways 'like a crab', abduction is increased. 'Hickory, dickory, dock', 'Clocks and watches' (or 'The grandfather's clock') or walking sideways with the therapist across the pool and back, the head and arms forward, have the same effect.

In supine lying, swaying the child from side to side with some rotation so that drag effect breaks the flexion pattern may prove helpful in creating more extension. The speed at which the child should be swayed can only be ascertained by working with each individual. A reversion to the flexion pattern on the part of the child means that one has swayed too fast and too hard.

Rotation in supine lying, as suggested for the hemiplegic, encourages extension and a more suitable shape for activity in water for the diplegic, but rolling to both sides must be employed. Where there is a marked asymmetry of the distribution of spasticity, more emphasis would be placed by the therapist on rotation away from that side, and resistance, when introduced, would be greater in order to bring about more extension in that side of the body.

The diplegic can be introduced by degrees to the prone position as favourable alterations in shape occur, and breathing control and the ability to submerge improve.

Among the therapeutic effects of activity in water are the relief of muscle spasm, development of relaxation and an increase in the range of joint movement. If activity takes place in a buoyancy-dominated situation where the effects of gravity are diminished, an increase in the creation of voluntary movement can be achieved. Therefore, all activities described under Ways and means (see p. 34) are of value, and changes of pace, of atmosphere and of mood are as important to the diplegic as to the child with any other condition.

Poor respiration and difficulties with communication are less likely to present problems in the diplegic child, but comprehension varies and perceptual problems may be present. However, the teaching of breathing control will improve respiration and mouth closure. Repetition of activities may be necessary where comprehension is poor. If the perceptual problems are those of poor body image and spatial awareness, these can be improved by those activities which involve extremes of posture and large movements of limbs. For example, 'Eggs for breakfast', 'Rag dolls' and other games where vertical rotation is the teaching point should be used, and for larger movements of the limbs 'Stars and stripes', 'Speedboats' and 'Making waves' are valuable.

All activities that have lateral rotation either in the vertical or horizontal plane as their teaching point will assist rotation around the longitudinal axis.

Individual work as well as group activities can be used with the diplegic child. Specific work on adductor spasticity and rotation can be introduced by the therapist standing between the child's legs as described for the hemiplegic child. 'Stepping stones' and 'Giant strides' will assist with improving gait. The use of turbulence to encourage stability against this disturbing force aids the diplegic with balance and counter-rotational control, but (as in other conditions) turbulence can be used to aid mobility.

The quadriplegic child

In children suffering from quadriplegic cerebral palsy, it is necessary to differentiate between those with spasticity and those with athetosis. While both will have alteration in shape, it will tend to be more fixed in the spastic and to fluctuate in the athetoid. The spastic quadriplegic child will therefore require activities which will assist in equalising dimensions of shape as much as possible. Strong adductor spasticity resulting in crossing of the legs will cause marked problems of lateral rotation and rolling around the longitudinal body axis. To control this rotation, the head, arms and legs can be used in activities directed at control in the vertical and horizontal planes. Examples of these activities are 'Passing the ring' (in the upright position and lying), 'Seaweed', 'Hallo', 'Rotating around the circle' (vertically, half lying and horizontally), 'Rolling onto the bar', 'Rolling from arm to arm', 'Resisted rolling' and 'The wheel'.

The athetoid whose posture, and therefore shape, is constantly fluctuating, needs to learn good blowing reactions and control of the head, arms and legs as soon as possible, thus giving the child a degree of control over the rotational movements that occur.

Respiration is usually explosive and poorly controlled in these children, and when head control is also poor, good blowing reactions will take a long time to acquire. Blowing should be in the background of all activities for all children, at all times, but acquires additional urgency with these children. Blowing is a means of bringing the head forward and therefore is an essential precursor to head control. For this action, games such as 'Bicycles', 'Bells', 'Eggs for breakfast', 'Charlie is over the water', 'Jumping', 'Rag dolls' and 'The wheels of the bus' are a few examples. Some of these activities bring in head control in the more stable 'ball' shape, others use the extremes of posture from 'ball' to 'stick', and all bring the head forward towards the water at some point in the activity when blowing can be encouraged.

Control of the arms and legs is needed, as, should any of the limbs come out of the water unexpectedly, the water will immediately try to balance the child's body according to the new shape. Thus though good head control is essential, if the arms and legs can be controlled, rotational problems are less likely to occur.

Awareness of and the need for control of the limbs can be achieved through activities such as 'lifting' water with hands and kicking it with the feet. Learning to splash with hands and feet or to make waves, stopping on command and staying still, is excellent for teaching this control. 'How wide? How tall?', patting the water in time to a song and jumping, walking sideways in a circle, 'Stepping stones', 'Giant strides' and 'Fairy strides' are further examples.

Spasticity and movement creation

In water, particularly in a buoyancy-dominated situation, or when the feet are not in contact with the bottom of the pool, the effect of gravity is diminished and therefore so is its effect on the postural mechanism. As a result, spasticity presents less of a problem.

The support of water helps relieve muscle spasm and gives freedom of movement not possible on land. However, responses to the demand to create a movement are slow and it is important that the child is given time to respond, whether this is to a blowing action or to the movement of limbs or trunk. Activities should, to a reasonable extent, be performed at the speed at which the children *can* respond. Changes of speed, atmosphere and pace are important in the programme, but time must be given for action on the part of the child.

Awareness of affected limbs can be assisted

through turbulent or drag effect. This effect is appreciated most at the distal end of the limbs, and consequently large movements which create greater turbulence are useful.

Since it is important that the child appreciates the necessity of keeping as much of the body in the water as possible, encouraging the child to 'lift' water in the cupped hand upwards through the water and feel the difference between below the surface and above is a useful means of introducing this concept.

Reduction of spasticity

Apart from the advantages of working in a buoyancy-dominated situation, rhythmic swinging, swaying and rolling actions reduce spasticity. Examples of activities that incorporate rhythmic swinging and swaying are 'Bells', 'Rag dolls', 'Seaweed', 'Hallo' and 'The grandfather's clock'. Those that incorporate rolling are 'Rolling from arm to arm', 'Rolling onto the bar' and simple gentle manual rolling facilitated by the therapist as in 'Little boats are on the sea'.

Reflex-inhibiting patterns assist in the reduction of spasticity and are easily incorporated into many activities. For instance, the child who has a predominantly extensor pattern of spasticity can be flexed into a 'ball' shape and held by the therapist (see p. 60). The child is held away from the therapist's body and gently rocked forwards and backwards. As with all activities, the child must be encouraged to blow as the face goes towards the water. Head control can also be acquired or improved in this exercise.

Where adductor spasm is a problem, the therapist can part the child's legs and stand between them as close to the knee level as possible. Support is given on the lateral side of the child's thighs and hips by the forearm and hands of the therapist. The child can then be swayed from side to side and also gently rotated (Fig. 42).

Fig. 42 *Hold for a child with adductor spasm.*

Adduction can be overcome by 'pendulum rocking'. The child is in the vertical position, facing the therapist, with outstretched hand on the therapist's shoulders. The therapist stabilises the child at the waist. The child is encouraged to part the legs sideways as far as possible and weight is transferred to one leg by a movement of the head and trunk to one side and then to the other in a rhythmic manner. Increasing abduction occurs as the child and therapist lean from side to side overcoming turbulent effect and leaning against the water. Where a child is unable to touch the bottom of the pool, the therapist's thighs provide a platform in the stable 'sitting' position and working at the same level as the child.

Where flexion is the predominant pattern of spasticity, every effort should be directed towards increasing extension through activities such as 'Rag dolls' and 'The wind, sun and rain' — in fact any which involve the extremes of posture moving from a long unstable 'stick' position to a stable 'ball' shape and then to a 'stick' again in supine lying. This pattern rhythmically repeated is valuable. The prone floating position, which might seem of use, presents formidable problems. It has been seen already that when the body is flexed, the tendency is for water to rotate that shape forwards and float it face down. Thus the flexed child in prone is likely to be rotated forward, and since extension of the head and spine will be limited, it is difficult for the child to achieve extension.

Athetosis, ataxia and control of movement

Water has a damping-down effect on movement, and for children with athetosis and ataxia this can be helpful. Keeping as much of the body in the water as possible is even more essential for these children, and teaching awareness and control of the limbs is extremely important.

Stability in water — always difficult to achieve — presents a special problem to the athetoid and ataxic. Involuntary movements further compound the difficulties, so the use of activities that begin in the more stable 'ball' shape and control the limbs are recommended, for example 'Bells' and 'Bicycles' performed on a one-to-one basis. As control develops, unrolling of the body can be employed, as in 'Rag dolls' and 'The wind, sun and rain'.

Frequently when taking the athetoid into water, head control and arm control are poor, especially in lying supine. The tendency is for the arms to be abducted asymmetrically and one arm or both to be above the surface of the water. Symmetry and control of the arms by the side of the body are desirable and are not achieved by the child without considerable difficulty.

It may be necessary to hold the head of the athetoid for brief periods to allow the child to get the arms to the side. As this movement is experienced it becomes easier to achieve and gradually the need to hold the head decreases. Once the arms are down, the child can be encouraged to hold a 12-

inch (30 cm) wooden stick with both hands, keeping this as low on the body as possible. If the child has difficulty in maintaining the grasp on this stick, the therapist can assist with the hands. Once more, if the hold is close to the centre of balance of the swimmer's body, symmetry can be maintained. The child's head rests on the therapist's shoulder and, should it have a tendency to turn to a particular side, the shoulder of choice will be the one on which the therapist's own head can control the tendency to turn.

When symmetry and control of the arms have been achieved in this manner, movements of the legs can be encouraged in rhythmical patterns. Demands to stop and lie still help gain control of the lower limbs. Impaired or absent head control requires constant attention and can be slowly and steadily improved in activities that encourage side-to-side, forward and backward and rotational head movements. Moving sideways in 'circle' games and appreciating that water has weight and can be leant against encourage side-to-side head movements. 'Bells', 'Bicycles', 'Eggs for breakfast', 'Reach for the bar' or 'Catching toes' will assist forward head control and control of the upper limbs. Turning or lateral rotational activities in the vertical and horizontal planes, such as 'Space ships', 'Turning in the arms', 'Passing a ring or ball' around the circle, 'Rolling from arm to arm' and, finally, moving around the circle independently will all demand head control, and so the child obtains the necessary skill in controlling the body.

Respiration and communication

It must be stated again that 'blowing' needs to be in the background of all activities and, with constant emphasis, the child may gain degrees of control.

Where the child has a poor cough reflex with a mouth constantly 'gagged open' and limited head control, the vertical position facing the therapist and supported by her below the axillae is the one of choice. To increase the child's control, the arms should be stretched forwards and the hands placed on the therapist's shoulders. This is often difficult for the child to achieve, but by modifying the hold the therapist can facilitate the position of the arms. Gentle assisted active kangaroo jumps with the commands 'jump' and 'blow' can introduce rhythm and control.

As mouth closure and head control improve, the child can be held vertically facing away from the therapist. It is important that the child stretches the arms forwards. Attainment of the supine lying position is gradually introduced, followed by recovery forwards to the vertical position.

Mario, an athetoid with marked fluctuations of tone but predominantly extensor in pattern, had poor head control and respiration, a mouth that gagged open and a depressed cough reflex. He was treated as suggested, and within six months it was possible, holding him in the vertical, to proceed through 30 feet (9 metres) of water with it lapping his mouth without his lips opening or his mouth filling with water. The speech therapist remarked on the ease with which he was now closing his mouth for speech and in feeding, and noted that his head was more controlled. It was almost two years before his breathing was such that taking him underwater was suggested. Mario was delighted. He was instructed to take a breath as he 'jumped' upwards and to 'blow' out as he submerged. These actions were achieved successfully several times without any coughing or problems with his respiration. A major milestone has been achieved and, since nothing succeeds like success, Mario was spurred to greater effort and the therapists were encouraged to develop his skills.

Postural tone

Poor or absent postural tone may be improved through activity in water. Water is a supportive medium and in the appropriate buoyancy-dominated situation — that is, a water depth over two-thirds a person's height — it is possible to encourage a more upright posture. Since shape can also be more readily altered in water and with less adverse stimulation of the anti-gravity muscles, improved posture can be obtained.

If turbulence is then introduced, the resultant actions taken by the swimmer to maintain stability become apparent in tone and posture. If the swimmer is required to move, a pause between each part of the pattern of movement demands greater postural control, balance and stability, and co-ordination can be developed.

Rotation

Many people with neurological problems lack rotation, particularly of the trunk, and this is a common problem in cerebral palsy. Lateral rotation around the longitudinal axis is easy to create in water and if it is facilitated, lateral rolling and rotation may be improved. Performed rhythmically both in the vertical and horizontal planes, rolling is a valuable adjunct to both therapeutic aims and the recreational aspects of water activity.

CONGENITAL ABNORMALITIES

When the child with a congenital abnormality is introduced to activity in water, the altered shape and density of the child's body must be studied. These factors will be different in each child and so an individual programme must be devised to assist the child in coping with the particular problem.

All activities are appropriate as a means of teaching the child the skills required for swimming.

However, the alterations in shape and density will almost certainly produce problems with rotational control laterally and vertically. Therefore early acquisition of this control is essential to the child's progress in water and should be emphasised at all times.

In particular, where a child has been born lacking full development of all four limbs, it is of paramount importance that rotational control is learned early and rapidly. The child will be dependent on head control both to create a forward and backward movement around the centre of buoyancy and to control very precisely the swing of the body, which will be a rapid one. This is so because in normal development the weight of the lower limbs has a braking effect. Without strong and accurate head control, the phocometic child may well be disturbed by this rapid movement.

In the same way, the child may fall forward in the water and need to rotate onto the back before creating a forward recovery to the upright position. The head must create the roll over the body by initiating strong lateral rotation. The act of rolling will also be prolonged in relation to the normal, so mental adjustments must be made and good breathing control established.

Once these children have mastered the necessary skills, they are able to move through water with a dolphin-like action and take considerable pleasure in the activity.

Rotational skills are equally important with either partial absence or deformity of a limb or limbs. But in these cases control of lateral and vertical rotation can be taught simultaneously. The ability to achieve the upright position may at times depend on a combination of gravitational and rotational effects, much as in the spina bifida child (see p. 202).

Children who have absence of the limbs can become excellent swimmers and may participate in many advanced aquatic skills.

MENTAL RETARDATION AND BEHAVIOUR DISORDERS

Children who are mentally retarded or have disorders of behaviour derive great benefit from activity in water and can learn many skills that carry over into their daily lives.

In the following pages, children with frank mental retardation are separated from those who have combined mental and physical handicaps. Children with specific behaviour disorders are dealt with under individual headings.

The child who is mentally handicapped has suffered an arrest in development so that intelligence is impaired and there is difficulty in learning and in adapting to society. In addition, due to particular perceptual disabilities, the child may well have difficulties in processing incoming information. In various ways these problems may be improved by activity in water.

In general, the deficit has been present from birth and the children are usually classified as profoundly retarded, severely retarded, moderately retarded, mildly retarded or borderline normal.

When taken into water, children with frank mental retardation do not present with the marked problems of altered shape and density we have seen in other disabilities. Their shape and density may be altered through fear, anxiety, tension, hyperactivity or complete disregard or lack of awareness of water and its characteristics, but this alteration in shape will not be seen in such an obvious manner as in the physically disabled.

The real problem facing the therapist is the level of comprehension of the swimmer. The individual's response to and translation of instructions will be directly related to enjoyment, effective use of water, and progress and safety.

The ultimate aim of water activity for these children must be, as in all handicaps, that the swimmer will be physically balanced, mentally adjusted and a safe participant in the medium. The best means of achieving this aim is through continuous repetition and reinforcement. The therapist will need considerable patience in maintaining the child's contact and interest and in developing the concentration span. Often this is achieved more effectively by working in groups with a one-to-one basis of swimmer and therapist or instructor.

Every skill must be learnt to a level at which it is performed completely automatically. This means that there must be a variety of activities used, all with the same teaching point, so that a splinter skill is not learnt. It is necessary that each skill is taught first in its primary form, then as a follow-up activity, and finally obliquely so that it is tested for the correct response. It must be demonstrated that the whole skill has been acquired and not just part of it.

Reactions to stressful conditions must be carefully observed. If the swimmer reacts appropriately, then the skill has been acquired. If an inappropriate reaction is demonstrated, the teaching of the skill must continue until such time as the correct response is shown.

All the games and activities that have been set out previously are applicable to the intellectually retarded child. Similarly, groups can be utilised for working with these children. The following points, however, are particularly applicable.

The group

The group can be formed of those with mixed handicaps and not necessarily only of children who are mentally retarded. Where it is not possible to combine physically handicapped and mentally retarded children, the group should be made up of children with differing levels of ability. Group members should stimulate one another and therefore the grouping of all severely mentally retarded together should be avoided, since interaction in such a group will tend to be poor and little progress can be expected.

Since some exceptions to grouping occur, these are discussed under the individual conditions.

Intellectual ability

The range of intellectual ability of the children who can benefit from and enjoy the water is enormously varied. The ability of the individual swimmer to translate instruction into action has to be understood, and the greatest care exercised by the therapist in ensuring that the action is correctly performed.

Some of these children are over-eager to participate and may be considered irresponsible, with no awareness of their actions and the possible consequences, while others show a lack of willingness to become involved either in the group or in responding to instructions.

Severely mentally retarded

Under this heading the ways in which profoundly retarded, severely retarded and moderately retarded children can be introduced to and taught basic skills in water are discussed.

The child who is profoundly affected will have gross retardation with delays in all areas of development. As the child matures, basic skills may develop and, with skillful training, the child may learn to use the limbs, walk, gain primitive speech and benefit from regular physical activity.

The severely retarded child will demonstrate obvious delays in motor development and communication but gradually develops motor skills, some understanding of speech and some response. The child's needs will include continuing direction and supervision, but such children usually conform to repetitive activities and routine which, in water, can be developed in the group and by using a large variety of games which have the same teaching point.

Motor development and speech are noticeably affected in the moderately retarded child, but simple communication, manual skills and safety habits can be taught on land and in water and many achieve the ability to swim, although they may always require a degree of supervision.

All of these children invariably show extremes of reaction to the water. There may be fear or no fear at all. The latter is more dangerous, and the children have to learn to respect water and acquire survival skills in addition to all the other aspects of swimming. It is necessary to help them achieve an understanding of varying water depths, recovery to a safe breathing position at all times and under all circumstances, and to ensure that they appreciate other risks such as those incurred by running around the bathside, which is usually wet. Under controlled conditions with experienced instructors, respect for the medium can be taught, but it is a slow process and every care must be taken to ensure that nothing untoward occurs that may set the learner back.

Others, less happy and extrovert, may have a fear of water and will need a period of time spent watching other children at play in the water. Gradually these children move closer to watch and are finally ready to join in. Introduction to the water must be allowed to happen in this way and should not be rushed. Occasionally it becomes necessary to bring the child in from a sitting position on the edge of the pool. Almost certainly a fuss will be made in this instance, but rapid involvement in an activity which is performed to a song that the child knows usually attracts the child's attention and further protestation is avoided, at least for a while.

While these children benefit from group work, there is also a place for individual handling, particularly when acquiring balance in all positions — walking, jumping, submerging and swimming. This individual emphasis can be stressed even within the group by the therapist who understands each child and any particular problems, so that the correct performance is ensured.

Mildly retarded and borderline normal

Children who are mildly retarded are usually slower than their normal peers to walk, feed themselves and talk, but can achieve practical skills and useful levels of academic and social skills while gaining a level of adequate self-maintenance.

Borderline normal children are near average in the acquisition of physical and self-help skills and gain academic, social and vocational skills that allow them to undertake semi-skilled, skilled or service occupations.

These children benefit greatly from activity in water and can become good swimmers. However, it is again of the utmost importance to ensure that the skills learned become completely automatic under all conditions and in all circumstances. The therapist must realise that there is a variation in understanding parts of the instruction, one part of a skill being readily absorbed, another part not understood. For example, in combined rotation the child may fall forward into the water and roll onto the back but fail to recover forward to a safe breathing position. It is then necessary to assist the child through the skill manually until certain that it has been acquired.

In the above example the therapist would manually 'fold' the body into a ball and then 'assist' extension to the upright standing position. Repetition of combined rotation with this manual assistance would be necessary with less assistance in creating the movements and holding the child for longer periods in each position until the child made active attempts to do the action independently.

There is frequently good physical ability and the children are usually happy extroverts. A noticeable feature is their persistence in repeating an action or skill they have acquired or found easy to perform, while evading the learning of new skills or those activities they find less appealing.

An example of this persistence can be cited in the case of an 8-year-old boy with Down's syndrome who could swim, albeit underwater. He would jump in at the shallow end, swim three strokes when he then needed to stand up and breathe. This sequence was repeated across the pool until he reached the other side. He then climbed out and jumped back in again to repeat the whole process. To break this habit and to ensure progress, an experienced instructor jumped into deep water with the child. Only when he could not find the bottom of the pool when needing to breathe did this child begin to understand about varying depths of water. Six jumps later he was swimming on the surface and went on quickly to swimming lengths of the pool.

Such persistence of part of an acquired skill should not be allowed to continue indefinitely. Progress and development should be ensured, and under controlled conditions with experienced personnel who understand the child's problems as well as the requirements of water activity, this can be achieved.

These children enjoy close personal contact and love to cling. They will take every opportunity to clasp the therapist closely, which impedes progress towards independence. Therefore entry and holds should be used at arm's length and clinging avoided.

Many of the children also avoid touching the bottom of the pool with their feet and, when participating in activities, will keep hips and knees flexed and hang on by the hands, thus being carried through an activity. By quickly dropping the hands, instructors can frequently bring about an effective reaction in the children, who lower their feet to find a point of contact with a surface and thus gain security. Without such attention to these details the children will not learn to disengage or control their bodies when acted upon by buoyancy and rotational forces, nor, indeed, will they learn to swim.

The responses of the Down's syndrome children need to be channelled appropriately and concentration maintained, and this is more readily achieved in a group situation. However, these children can quite unexpectedly disrupt the group and should be quietly withdrawn by their instructor to a part of the pool where the inappropriate behaviour can be channelled into activities such as vigorous 'kangaroo jumps' or kicking and splashing then stopping and lying still on command, repeated several times. This can bring the situation under control, thus allowing the swimmer and the instructor to rejoin the group.

Autistic children (behaviour disorder)

Autism is an uncommon developmental disorder of childhood. Stone (1976, p.66) cites Leo Kanner in 1943 as first drawing attention to the disorder, which he termed early infantile autism. Kanner delineated three presenting clinical features.

1. A lack of awareness of people, an avoidance of ordinary contact with others, an 'alone-ness' which is what autism really means.
2. Abnormalities in the development of speech varying from unusual forms of syntax to the extremes of complete mutism.
3. An 'obsessional desire for sameness' — that is, a tendency to become acutely distressed when an accustomed arrangement is disturbed.

The label 'autistic' has been applied rather loosely to a variety of developmental disorders. Stone (1976) suggests that autism should be restricted to cases presenting the syndrome as described by Kanner, recognising that this is not a common condition and that more frequently a variety of clinical states showing autistic features is encountered.

The 'alone-ness' is an aspect of these children that can be avoided by contact with the therapist and by working in a group situation, though these ideals are not always easy to achieve.

The situation where the autistic child is left alone in water and ignored must be rigorously avoided. The author has seen such children left in this way with their hands close to their faces, rocking forwards and backwards, circling continuously and making their way into deeper and deeper water, 'alone' in their world and totally unaware of the danger.

They generally love the feel of water and have a good response to rhythm, thus the use of games and activities to music and, above all singing which frequently brings about their first verbal responses, is an excellent way in which to work with them.

Like the Down's syndrome children, the autistic child can suddenly go wild and disrupt the group. This should be dealt with as it arises in the same way as for the Down's syndrome child.

The hyperkinetic syndrome

Graham (1977) suggests overactivity in children arises for a variety of reasons, and that the level of activity is partly determined as a temperamental characteristic. However, he states that severe overactivity may occur as part of a poorly differentiated cluster of symptoms in which, in the absence of severe social stress (and in addition to overactivity), there may be impersistence, lack of concentration, short attention span, distractibility, impulsiveness and lack of social inhibition.

Not all these problems are present all the time, and vary from situation to situation. Hyperkinetic behaviour can be improved through activity in water. Drag effect, the weight of water and the extra energy required to move in water have a dampening effect on movement for these children which can be used to advantage in teaching more acceptable behaviour.

Graham (1977) suggests that they are very responsive to environmental situations. People taking them into water should note the activities which suit the children best. These activities may need to change from individual to group work depending on the child's reaction at any time. Thus, the programme needs to be flexible.

The overall mastery of the act of swimming with controlled rhythmic movement appears to have a beneficial effect upon hyperkinetic children.

PERCEPTUAL DISABILITIES

The perceptual disabilities discussed here are spatial awareness, body image, difficulty in estimating size, distance, time and depth, perseveration and concentration.

Spatial awareness

Examples of activities that improve a child's ability to locate the position of objects in space and enable accurate movement are 'How wide? How tall?', 'Eggs for breakfast', 'Ring a ring O' roses' and similar circle activities, 'Kangaroo jumps' and 'Stepping stones'.

When working in a circle, it is not necessary to move continually sideways. The circle can be made smaller by walking or jumping towards the centre, and larger by moving backwards. Comments on the size of the circle help reinforce spatial awareness, and emphasis on the position of the head when walking forwards or backwards is important. In order for the feet to remain down in the vertical plane, the head should be kept forward, whether walking forwards or backwards. The children, with the assistance of a therapist, can at first make their way around the bar. Care must be taken that they become aware of the point at which their vertical balance becomes critical — at a water level of two-thirds their height. Thus they learn about gravity-dominated shallower water and buoyancy-dominated deeper water.

Body image

Children who have poor body image can be made increasingly aware of themselves through activities which involve the extremes of posture, which require control of their arms and legs, and in which greater turbulence is created.

Activities which involve the extremes of posture are all the 'ball' and 'stick' games, that is those used for vertical rotation and consisting of total patterns of flexion and extension (Reid, 1976). 'Eggs for breakfast', 'Reach for an object', 'Rag dolls', 'The wind, sun and rain' are a few examples.

To encourage control of the limbs, 'How wide? How tall?', lifting up the water with the hands or kicking it with the feet, will help give an awareness of the weight of water. Splashing with hands or feet and stopping on command, making waves with the arms and legs in games such as 'Stars and stripes', in both standing and in lying, encourage control and awareness of the limbs. Turbulent or drag effect is most noticeable at the distal part, and the child can be made aware of the length of the limbs and the dimension of the body reach and span. 'Simon says' and games that involve hiding feet and hands in different ways are also useful. As the child acquires this control, the arm and leg actions for appropriate strokes may be introduced along with good breathing control — both requisites for swimming.

Size, distance, time and depth

Activities which will help reduce the difficulties in estimating size and distance are those that encourage the children to curl up in a 'ball' and extend to a 'stick', changing the circle size from small to large and changing from a short arm hold to a long arm hold as they move in and out. Games involving equipment, such as 'Pieces of eight' in which various sized objects are used, are valuable. Jumping from one object to another, 'Fairy strides' and 'Giant strides' are other useful activities.

Time estimation can be encouraged through rhythm and the use of songs and music and spoken rhyme where the beat is strongly emphasised.

Estimation of depth is involved in entry and exit, whether this is down the steps or ramps or over the side. It is reinforced also by working from shallow to deeper water and in submerging and trying to touch the bottom.

Perseveration

Children who have difficulty in changing from one task to another can be helped by appropriately planned programmes of activity in water. The programme should have changes of pace from slow to fast, changes of atmosphere from quiet to noisy, changes of mood from seriousness to laughter, and changes of shape, not only from 'ball' and 'stick' and their own body shapes, but in the formation in which the activities are performed and linked together in the programme.

Concentration

It may seem that children who are easily distracted, especially by sound or movement in their surroundings, are not suited to programmes of activity in water.

Pools tend to be noisy areas where shouting, laughter and splashing, combined with active movement on the part of the swimmers and the constant movement of the water, can have a distracting and disturbing effect. However, working in groups has been found to assist concentration over longer time spans. As the child's attention is focused on the group and the other children and their achievements, increased awareness and motive follow. This can be encouraged further by the introduction of more competition in the games.

THE CLUMSY CHILD

Clumsy children demonstrate problems in motor skills that are out of keeping with their general abilities. The majority also have learning difficulties, and the combination leads to the children failing in many areas. As a result, behavioural and emotional factors arise.

Programmes for the acquisition of motor skills have been used to help the clumsy child but these have been almost entirely land based.

Arnhem and Sinclair (1979) suggested that water activity introduced the clumsy child to a new dimension, and stated that if water was used appropriately, it could enhance the physical and perceptual training of such children. Campbell (1978) described a combined programme of land-based and water-based activities. The philosophy is based on the link between the prenatal fluid environment of the fetus and the similar fluid environment of the pool (especially where the water is warm) and all the other advantages of the medium such as buoyancy and ease of movement.

The games and activities which have already been described have proved valuable in the treatment of clumsy children and may be adapted to augment the programmes propounded by Arnhem and Sinclair (1979) and Campbell (1975). Such items as:

(a) breathing control,
(b) body image and spatial awareness,
(c) balance and co-ordination,
(d) sequencing,
(e) laterality and directionality,
(f) endurance and strength,
(g) swimming ability,
(h) social skills,
(i) speech and language,

should be included in the programme.

Activities can be developed by the use of equipment — balls, hoops, ropes, dive rings, discs, sticks and bricks, play tubes and other inflatable toys. Awareness of body image can be increased by adapting the activity 'If you're happy and you know it', by the use of 'Simon says' and similar games. Laterality may be taught in games such as

'Looby Loo' or the 'Hokey cokey', and directionality when moving around or to one side of objects. Ropes and other items are valuable when developing spatial awareness. The children can go over and under in many different ways. Obstacle courses, sequences for memorising the retrieval of dive rings, the use of coloured hoops and other toys are just some of the ways in which sequencing and memory skills may be trained.

Breathing control and swimming ability should be checked at the commencement of the programme and recorded. During the sessions these skills can be progressed by timing the children swimming either widths or lengths or interesting them in improving their own times. Endurance and strength will also benefit.

A programme of activity in water appeals to these children, and those who at first appear timid and lacking in confidence do develop skills in the water quite rapidly, with a resulting alteration in attitude. For many, an aquatic programme in itself is a morale booster. Water is a great leveller and thus they are able to participate with less awareness of their failings.

The manner in which land-based motor skill training programmes are conducted applies to the water activity sessions. The parents should be informed about all aspects of the activities and the author has found it invaluable to have mothers or fathers recording swimming times and other achievements on the bathside, as the presence of the therapist is necessary in the water throughout the pool sessions.

The progress of the children can only be measured if accurate recording is undertaken on each occasion and the results transferred to appropriate charts which should be kept for each child.

The proper orientation of the children to the pool and pool area is important, and all safety rules should be both explained and enforced at all times.

Water has much to offer the clumsy child, just as for the vast majority of normal people. The appropriate and specific use of water can aid the development of a child who is falling behind his peers, and thereby confidence, self-respect and emotional behaviours improve in addition to gross and fine motor skills.

HEAD INJURY

The number of people sustaining head injuries has increased steadily in recent years. These injuries can arise from accidents on the road, during participation in sport, in the home and in industry (Jennett and Teasdale, 1981). Whatever the cause or type of head injury, people who survive the accident are frequently left with a number of problems that affect function and require prolonged treatment.

It is beyond the scope of this book to discuss the different types of head injury. The problems which result from the injury are numerous, complex and tend to change in nature over time. They can be physical, emotional, intellectual and behavioural and they may include changes in personality, difficulty in controlling emotion, and varying degrees of intellectual impairment. In particular, people taking head-injured persons into water need to be aware of the sudden and sometimes violent fluctuations in emotion which can occur. In spite of this, hydrotherapy has a part to play in the treatment of the head injured in the subacute phase when consciousness begins to improve, just as swimming programmes may prove useful in providing stimulation as well as a regular means of activity and exercise in the later stages of rehabilitation.

The subacute phase

The aims of treatment in this phase are:

(a) to reduce spasticity and promote relaxation,
(b) to encourage movement.
(c) to improve head control,
(d) to improve respiration and breathing control,
(e) to develop stability, balance and co-ordination,
(f) to re-educate functional activities.

The specific contraindication to hydrotherapy for the head-injured person in the subacute phase is lack of continence. One of the criteria for treatment is that the person remains continent for a period of two hours. In some instances there is a requirement that the person wears some form of protective garment beneath the swimwear. This criterion is the one required at the Royal Perth (Rehabilitation) Hospital, Perth, Western Australia. Open wounds that cannot be covered and any known infection would contraindicate pool therapy. The presence of a tracheostomy need not preclude treatment in the water provided a complete seal can be achieved over the opening.

The head-injured person will enter the water by means of a hoist with a stretcher. In some cases it is helpful to place a horse-shoe-shaped flotation collar around the neck while the person is still on the hoist. This may be necessary when head control is extremely poor, when the therapist feels that this will assist in handling, or when it is intended to use further flotation equipment. The head is supported and controlled, thus allowing the therapist to attach pelvic and ankle floats more readily.

An explanation of the treatment will have been given to the person prior to entry, but it is essential to reiterate this once the person is in the water. Throughout the treatment session, the therapist should explain the activities, the reasons for performing them, encourage participation and acknowledge achievements however small. One of the problems that is a consequence of head injury is that of increased tone. This is usually distributed throughout the body — that is, the head, trunk and limbs are affected. The distribution is rarely symmetrical, one side of the body being more affected than the other, or the muscle tone of one side of the body may be qualitatively different from that of the other side. These factors will have considerable bearing on the balance of the person's body in the water and therefore one of the first acts the therapist should carry out is that of studying shape and assessing balance of the body in the supine lying position. Once this has been done, the person must be instructed as to how to overcome and control the rotational effects. This invariably requires rotation of the head away from the side to which the body is rolling, and the head should be maintained in that position.

The density of the head-injured person appears to increase. Certainly a greater number of head-injured people tend to sink rather than float. Part of the explanation may lie in the fact that the head injuries are frequently sustained by that age group — between 18 and 36 years approximately — in which the relative density of the body is close to the relative density of water. In other words, the age of the person and density of the body, even prior to the injury, were such that flotation would not have been achieved easily.

While the therapist is supporting the person in supine lying, it is advisable to attempt to reduce spasticity and induce relaxation. This may be achieved by swaying the body laterally. The hold will be the backing hold (see p. 55) but may require the therapist's hands to be placed beyond the waist towards the hips and for them to be placed on the sides of the body. This gives the therapist better control and leverage as the body is swayed from side to side through the water. The swaying movement is a lateral one, but at times a rotational component may be added towards the end of each swaying action. There are no firm guidelines for the speed, direction and manner of this swaying action. The therapist must work this out on the basis of individual responses, which will be specific to the person on any particular day. Thus, it requires constant observation and evaluation of the effects of the swaying action. Any adverse responses which occur, such as an increase in spasticity, indicate that the swaying action needs to be modified or temporarily withdrawn.

The upper trunk may be swayed from side to side and rotated to reduce spasticity. The therapist stands between the person's legs. The elbows are placed on the outer side of the person's knees, the forearms along the lateral borders of the thighs and the hands over the hips. The head is supported by the inflated collar. Once again the range of sway, the speed and the particular direction are adjusted to the individual being treated. Small automatic postural effects can be induced by the judicious and appropriate use of this swaying action.

A large proportion of head-injured people demonstrate problems of extension; others may have a pattern of flexion. Although it might seem unwise to place the person in supine lying, the position in which increased extensor tone is present (Brodal, 1981; Heiniger and Randolph, 1981), the buoyancy of the water and reduced effects of gravity make this position less inappropriate. Where flexion is the problem, extension can be developed in the supine lying position using the modified backing hold and swaying the body laterally with rotation so that the legs cannot be maintained in such marked flexion against the weight of water and the drag effect of turbulence.

Following induction of some degree of relaxation, it is then necessary to develop breathing control. This is not an easy task and requires time and patience from the therapist and the head-injured person. Instruction should begin with the first session and be practised throughout all future sessions. The therapist must communicate to the person the role that breathing control has in achieving and maintaining balance, relaxation and safety, as well as in respiratory function, oro-facial function and speech. The first sounds may result from the attempts to blow, closure of the mouth against the water may become habitual and improved respiratory function may result when the movements of the chest are alternately facilitated and resisted by the pressure of the water around the chest (see p. 8). The speech therapist plays a large part in the rehabilitation of the head injured and, in the author's experience, it has proved invaluable to consult with the speech therapist and, when possible, attendance at the pool sessions, especially in the early stages of rehabilitation, on the part of speech therapist enhances this aspect of treatment.

Breathing control is important when lying supine in the water but it is extremely difficult to teach when the person is in this position. A sitting position is required initially and this may be achieved from the supine lying position in two ways. If the person already has some ability to sit on land, the therapist may remain behind the swimmer, supporting at the waist, and instruct the person to bring the head and arms forward at the same time as flexing the hips and knees. If the therapist's body has been stabilised against the wall of the pool and a stable sitting position has been adopted, the person can sit on the therapist's thighs. In the second method the therapist should move to the side of the person and support under the trunk just below the lower border of the scapulae with one arm and under the thighs with the other. The person is given the same instruction as previously, but in this position the therapist is able to facilitate the action. If a second therapist is available, it is possible for one to work from behind or at the side and the other to be a focal point for the person to work towards. A rail at the side of the pool can also be useful when working alone. A small floating object that can be blown across the surface helps the person to focus in midline and encourages the blowing action. As some control is gained, attempts may be made to blow into the water.

Gross patterns of flexion and extension of the whole body are gained in teaching the person to come to the sitting position and lie back again. The emphasis should be on the control of the head, both in coming erect and lying back. With a person demonstrating marked extension, the pattern of flexion and the sitting position would be accentuated — the reverse where flexion was predominant.

Head control should also be taught as part of lateral rotation. While rolling through 360° is not usually possible at this stage, head control can be encouraged in the manner described in 'Resisted rolling' (p. 142). 'Rolling on to the bar' (p. 140) and 'Rolling arm to arm' (p. 146) are the best activities to employ when commencing teaching rolling through 360°.

Any mobility of the upper and lower limbs should be encouraged. The person may be placed in flotation equipment and permitted to move around the pool using any movement possible. Where one arm or leg moves more easily than the other, the person will tend to progress in circles. Therefore the action of the better limbs should be modified, and passive, then assisted active, movements applied in the appropriate range to the more affected limbs, especially the arm, by the therapist.

Activity in the vertical should be developed. However, it is essential to introduce the upright position carefully, particularly in those persons who are generally recumbent or semi-recumbent. Standing either supported by the therapist from in front or behind, or holding on to the rail, should be undertaken in deeper water. Transference of weight sideways and later walking sideways should be commenced first. Later, step standing, transference of weight forwards and backwards and walking forwards are introduced.

If increased spasticity should occur during any activity while treatment is taking place, it is advisable to return to the supine lying position and begin lateral swaying to regain relaxation. This may be required several times in any one pool session.

As the person progresses, an increasing number of activities are introduced, especially those described under the sections for rotational control and balance and co-ordination.

Rehabilitation phase

The aims of treatment for this phase are:

(a) to reduce spasticity where present, and to maintain and improve relaxation,
(b) to encourage greater mobility and independence,
(c) to maintain and improve head control,
(d) to maintain and increase respiration and breathing control,
(e) to maintain and improve stability, balance and co-ordination,
(f) to promote greater functional ability,

(g) to develop dynamic exercise and swimming ability.

During this rehabilitative phase, activity in water should become less of an individual occupation. The person should be introduced to group work, as not only does this provide greater motivation and stimulation, but it also encourages socialisation. All of the activities described in the text are of value at this stage, and every effort should be made to ensure that the head-injured person's activities are directed towards independent functioning in the water: this includes safety in swimming, on the poolside and in the changing areas.

For those head injured whose consciousness has returned but who remain severely affected — chair-bound in either sitting or half-lying — activities should be carried out in groups. The person may have been discharged home or into care, and water activity in the hydrotherapy pool may no longer be possible on a regular basis. The swimming club that caters for the disabled can offer a suitable alternative, especially the club that numbers a physiotherapist amongst its members. The therapist can act as an adviser to those who would work in the water with the person to the advantage of both swimmer and club helpers.

The author has seen marked changes in attitude and effort on the part of the head injured when enabled to work in a group and club situation. Whenever possible, independent floating and swimming with whatever mobility the person possesses should be developed. The joy and freedom of independent movement that can be achieved in water when such movement is difficult or impossible on land should not be denied those who remain severely disabled.

EPILEPSY

Epilepsy is described as a disturbance of cerebral function produced by recurrent abnormal discharges of neurons. It takes a number of different forms, and is frequently accompanied by loss of consciousness (Lance and McLeod, 1975). The clinical effects depend on and are determined by the location and duration of the discharge.

Farmer (1975) indicates that the most frequently seen seizure in children is that of a febrile convulsion which occurs in association with fevers and acute systemic infections. Epileptic attacks, however, can occur in people of any age, any background and any level of intellect. Epilepsy is frequently found in conjunction with other conditions such as cerebral palsy — approximately half of the children having this condition, particularly those who are hemiplegic or quadriplegic, also suffer from epilepsy. Differing views are held as to whether activity in water is suitable for those with epilepsy. Burden and Schurr (1976) indicate that epileptics can be allowed to swim as long as appropriate supervision is provided. In the case of children, the agreement of the parents and the child's doctor should be sought prior to commencing swimming. The adult swimmer should also have medical permission. The author does not wish to argue for or against the inclusion of the epileptic in water activity programmes, but does suggest that if approached to take a known epileptic into the pool, certain factors must be ascertained and precautions taken.

For the person who is an epileptic and has no other complicating factors, swimming can be taught by any method. However, the instructor must have obtained the following information.

1. Are there any warning signs when a seizure is about to occur?

2. Is the swimmer on any medication for the seizures?

3. Are the seizures well controlled by this medication?

4. How frequently does the swimmer take the medication and what are the times of administration?

5. The state of health of the swimmer at each attendance.

The warning signs or aura should be known to all concerned. If the swimmer is on medication, the instructor should check when the last dose was administered and ascertain the state of health at each attendance. Should the swimmer have failed to take the prescribed drugs or indicate in any way that the general state of health is lower than is usually the case, then activity in water should be postponed on that day.

It is interesting to note that epileptic seizures are uncommon in water. The author, in discussion with specialists in the treatment of epilepsy, has been informed that provided undue excitement and tension are avoided, and any factors such as flickering lights and reflections on the water are eliminated, a fit is unlikely to occur.

It is also important that facilities are available for coping with an attack and that experienced personnel are on hand to assist in the event of a fit occurring. It is essential that all personnel should be aware of the measures to be undertaken. Although appropriate measures have been laid down by a number of statutory bodies, these do tend to vary throughout the world.

At all times the swimmer suffering from epilepsy should be carefully watched. The author believes this can be carried out diligently but unobtrusively. It would appear more advantageous to allow the epileptic to swim under controlled conditions with efficient and knowledgeable personnel on hand than to refuse to allow such a person to swim. In the author's experience, such a refusal has led to a situation where the person has chosen not to divulge the presence of the condition in order to be permitted to join in a swimming class. This is potentially dangerous for the sufferer and could lead to serious or even fatal consequences.

The epileptic who, between convulsions, is usually fit and normal, will not present marked alterations in shape and density. The problem of balance in water will be slight, just as it is in the able-bodied population. However, when epilepsy is associated with cerebral palsy, the altered shape and density due to the primary condition must be taken into consideration.

When working on a one-to-one basis and with the knowledge not only that the swimmer suffers from epilepsy, but also the nature of the warning and of the aura, the situation can be managed well. Although the epileptic may be able to swim, the condition warrants a continued one-to-one ratio.

It is in the interests of safety for everyone that if the epileptic cannot swim the skill should be learned, since individuals, particularly children, already incur many restrictions in their lives. Much, however, depends on the type of fit and the frequency of the attacks. The social and psychological benefits of swimming have already been stated and are equally applicable to the epileptic. Risks are part of activity in water for all persons; for the epileptic it is the sudden and unpredictable nature of the attacks that adds to the risks (National Co-ordinating Committee on Swimming for the Disabled, 1975). If the precautions stated in the text are taken, the risks can be minimised and the epileptic gains in many ways from learning to swim.

ASTHMA

When swimming programmes for asthmatics were introduced some 20 years ago, it was known that exercise induced asthma in most sufferers. At that time there was no scientific evidence to prove that swimming was more or less likely to provoke an attack (Lindsay, 1979). Since then, research has been undertaken and has provided evidence both supporting swimming as an excellent activity for the asthmatic (Fitch and Morton, 1971; Fitch, 1978; Oseid *et al.*, 1978), and indicating that a re-examination of the results of swimming for asthmatics might suggest a need for the development of other types of exercise programmes (Phelan, 1980). However, the important psychological advantages accruing from swimming programmes have been noted by critics and advocates alike.

Oseid *et al.* (1978) suggest that the physical treatment of asthmatic children is directed towards controlling attacks through relaxation, breathing exercises, postural drainage and specific efforts to correct chest deformities. Oseid and his colleagues (1978) are not alone in indicating that appropriately planned programmes are beneficial and that improved exercise tolerance and breathing control can result (Fitch, 1978; Shepherd, 1980). Fitch (1978) maintains that swimming is an excellent exercise to restore and maintain fitness in many conditions, including asthma, and sees it as valuable not only for rehabilitation but also for recreation and sport.

For the asthmatic child who requires treatment over a prolonged period of time, an activity that is of interest and stimulating, yet at the same time improves the physical condition should prove vaulable in several ways. Swimming programmes can include underwater activity, improve breathing control and physical development. The development of secondary chest deformities can also be prevented by performance of correct stroking techniques. Perhaps of equal significance though are the social and psychological benefits which undoubtedly improve the quality of life enjoyed by the asthmatic.

Physiotherapists who are deeply involved in the treatment of asthmatic children may well be faced with the task of taking such children into water. Familiarisation with the element can be carried out in the manner already described (see p. 7). The emphasis on breathing control in all the activities is of major importance. The asthmatic child may learn to swim quickly, particularly as no marked changes in shape will be evident. However, small alterations may be present and these should be observed and evaluated and a balanced position developed. Correct positioning for stroking (p. 184) is critical, not only because the child may wish to participate in competitive swimming programmes, but also as a means of improving physical development and preventing deformities of the thoracic region.

BURNS

Hydrotherapy, in the strict sense of the word, has a part to play in the treatment of burns. Behrend (1963) points out the value of the Hubbard tank with water in motion for debridement, and an appropriate temperature of about 38°C (100.4°F). Shepherd (1980) indicates that debridement may be carried out non-traumatically in the bath, the whirlpool effects and active movements helping the process, facilitating the removal of dressings and reducing infections. Capillary ingrowth is also improved. The temperature suggested by Shepherd (1980) is three degrees lower than that advocated by Behrend (1963). Shepherd (1980) gives useful advice on general procedures for the burnt child and her book should be consulted if it is planned to use hydrotherapy in these cases. It should be noted that the effects of burns on a child's emotional well-being are enormous, and the child may be in a highly anxious state at the prospect of hydrotherapy. Bernstein (1976) cautions as to the possible effects on the child and others of the burned parts of the body and the sight of charred flesh becoming detached in the water.

If at all possible, the child should not only be gently informed as to all the procedures undertaken and their purpose, but diversions such as toys and music should be available to relieve anxiety. At all events, the child must be treated with consideration and allowances made for extreme swings in behaviour and attitude during the bath sessions.

Later, when newly grafted sites have healed, gentle active movements in water may be permitted. Very much later, when healing has taken place and the child is returned to living as normal a life as possible, swimming may form part of the activities the child engages in and which help not only to maintain function generally, but also to institute obvious social and psychological recovery.

INFECTIONS OF THE CENTRAL NERVOUS SYSTEM

Infections of the brain, spinal cord and peripheral nerves may result from a variety of causes, and while many children do recover from the effects of the inflammation of these structures, some are left with permanent neurological damage. It is these latter children that the physiotherapist may be called upon to treat in the water. Examples of conditions in which hydrotherapy has a part to play in the stage of recovery include anterior poliomyelitis and Guillain–Barré syndrome.

Anterior poliomyelitis

This is an acute infection caused by a virus which destroys the motor cells of the anterior horn of the spinal cord and brainstem. The initial influenza stage of the illness is followed by paralysis of the muscles of a flaccid motor neuron type. The paralysis is usually widespread to begin with, but as considerable recovery takes place, the person is left with some residual asymmetrical paralysis of certain muscle groups.

The aims of treatment are to:

(a) prevent contractures,
(b) maintain the circulation,
(c) strengthen the affected muscles.

Activity in water will assist with all these aims. However, since pain is a symptom of the condition and the muscles have been tender to the touch, the child may be extremely anxious about movement when allowed out of bed. If the child can understand, it may be explained that the warmth and buoyancy of the water will make it easier to move. For the younger child, such explanations are not feasible and overcoming fear will require time and patience. In both instances the pool sessions should be conducted gently and made as enjoyable as possible.

There will in these children be marked alterations in shape and density due to the effects of the disease, the asymmetrical nature of the flaccid paralysis and the loss of density, all of which will produce rotational effects and body parts that will float easily. Careful observation of these effects must be made, and the treatment programme chosen will reassure the child and teach control of these effects.

Passive movements may be given to prevent contractures, and the warmth of the water will allow these procedures to be carried out more easily than on land, but great care must be exercised. Active movements should be encouraged and the fullest range of movement obtained. Buoyancy will both assist and resist movement and the exercise programme should be planned accordingly and the progressions carefully graded. As with all activity in water for children, the exercises are best carried out in the form of games.

Re-education of walking may be commenced in the water. The appropriate depth is important: the water should cover the child's shoulders in the vertical position as this assists the maintenance of an upright posture, the water providing support around the whole body. To encourage balance and stability, turbulence may be placed around the body (see p. 176). Initially, however, the therapist will need to use the facing hold (see p. 53). The procedures for re-educating gait have been described (see p. 189), and may be followed for children with anterior poliomyelitis commencing with transference of weight sideways. An alternative method of teaching weight transference and walking sideways is that of working in a group in a circle formation. The preferred hold would then be across the back (see p. 56), at least in the early stages of the activity.

Other activities such as jumping, hopping, skipping and dancing can be undertaken in deeper water, encouraging increased movement. The buoyancy of the water allows this without undue weight-bearing. In addition, these actions provide interest and psychological benefits for the child. As improvement occurs, the child should work in shallower water with increasing gravity effects. Balance and co-ordination can be increased if, instead of walking and jumping continuously, a pause is introduced between each phase of walking and between each jump. The turbulence created by the forward movement will disturb the body's balance. The child should pause for as long as is required to stabilise the body before moving again. The ways in which a stabilised position may be obtained are given in the description of the re-education of walking (see p. 189).

The Bad Ragaz techniques (see p. 200) may be of interest to the older child who can understand what is required and become intrigued by the pattern of movement required. For the younger child, these techniques are of little value and the therapist's ingenuity will be taxed to encourage similar movements in another form. As respiratory function may have been affected by the disease, the importance of breathing control and the need to improve respiration are evident.

As with all children in connection with activity in water, the therapist must watch for signs of fatigue or the effects of cold. A warm pool is essential, but it should be neither too warm nor too cool. The former will be enervating and the latter will inhibit muscular activity. The temperatures already advocated are suitable for the treatment in water of the child suffering from anterior poliomyelitis.

Guillain–Barré syndrome and peripheral nerve lesions

This syndrome is a form of peripheral neuropathy, the cause of which is unknown although it may follow a viral infection of the gastrointestinal or upper respiratory tract. The disorder affects both motor nerves and those of sensation and the person may have difficulty in moving, breathing, swallowing, talking and smiling, as well as some numbness, paraesthesia and loss of sense of position. Pain is a feature of the condition and varying degrees of weakness and paralysis commence in the lower limbs and spread to the upper limbs. The person is hospitalised and management is symptomatic. Physical treatment is similar to that for poliomyelitis and would, in both the intermediate and ongoing stages of rehabilitation, include pool therapy.

The condition gradually resolves itself, the strength of muscles returning in an ascending order. Assessment of muscle power is carried out on land and the Modified Oxford Scale for Water can be employed for hydrotherapy evaluation. Pool programmes would follow that outlined for anterior poliomyelitis, but, owing to the symmetrical distribution, there is less likelihood of alterations in shape. Density will be affected but this will alter as recovery takes place.

The aims of hydrotherapy are to:

(a) increase muscle power,
(b) improve respiratory function,
(c) increase the range of movement,
(d) improve the circulation.

Passive movements may be given to all joints to prevent stiffness of contractures, though in the case of children such movements may be inappropriate. The anxiety engendered by the pain experienced in the early stages of the disease and the understandable fear of being handled make it more suitable to employ assisted active or active movements. Games that will encourage activity in as full a range of movement as possible should be used. The games provide a means of distraction for the child, who usually produces greater movement as a result, and this in turn may be of more value than Bad Ragaz or other very specific techniques. As recovery takes place, careful grading of the progression of exercise is essential.

The points made regarding fatigue and cold are as valid for this condition as for other peripheral nerve lesions. For all conditions where circulation may be affected — for example a peripheral nerve lesion, spina bifida and cerebral palsy — care should be taken that the feet are not damaged by dragging on the pool floor. The wearing of socks will help to prevent abrasions and injuries of this kind.

In dealing with peripheral nerve lesions, it should be remembered that the treatment programme and the progressions will vary with the extent of nerve involvement. Therapeutic exercise and recreational activity have considerable value in both the stages of recovery and final rehabilitation of these disorders.

APPENDIX

THE CRIBRIFORM PLATE

The cribriform plate is the horizontal component of the ethmoid bone in the central anterior portion of the base of the skull, with a central crest — the crista galli — dividing it into right and left portions. The plate is penetrated by numerous foramina (or holes), through which passes the olfactory nerve. This is the 1st cranial nerve, the nerve of smell arising from the olfactory bulb situated at the anterior part of the base of the brain and which innervates the olfactory mucosa of that region. In addition, there is at least one slit on either side of the crista galli into which dips the dura mater (part of the meninges), the membrane which encloses the brain and the spinal cord. On the nasal side these slits have a covering of very fine nasal olfactory epithelium. Therefore, any infection introduced into the upper reaches of the nasal cavity can involve the nasal mucous membrane and consequently, through the various foramina, the dura mater, the olfactory nerve, the base of the brain and thence to the spinal cord. Not only infections but chemicals, either in solution or gaseous form, can produce unpleasant effects as well as damage to the delicate mucous membrane. Such effects can occur to the tissues in the adult form. In the infant whose tissues are still developing, the trauma is likely to be more devastating.

THE EAR

The ear is divided into three clearly defined compartments — the outer ear (or externa), the middle ear (or media), and the inner ear (or interna). With the exception of the interna, these are connected to the outside.

The outer ear consists of that part of the ear from the auricle, seen on the outside of the skull, to the ear drum (or tympanic membrane). In the neonate and infant, the 'ear hole' (the external auditory meatus) is virtually non-existent and the ear drum itself is on the outside of the skull surrounded by a bony ring known as the tympanic ring. It is hardly necessary in the infant to move the external ear in order to see the ear drum, and infections causing autis externa, chemicals, water pressure or the careless poking of an object into the external auditory meatus can be dangerous and cause damage to delicate tissues. In the adult whose external auditory meatus is well developed with a definite 'S'-shaped curve, protective hairs and wax, the ear drum is far less likely to be damaged. A bubble of air is frequently trapped in the ear before any liquid reaches the ear drum itself. The formation of the adult ear is not complete until the fifth year of life.

The middle ear is a cavity inside the ear drum and consists of three minute bones known as the ossicles. These are activated by the ear drum (tympanic membrane), and multiply the vibrations to the sensors of the inner ear. The cavity of the middle ear is filled with air through the auditory tube (the nasopharynx), which originates at the back of the throat and nose. Any infection of the throat can pass, or be forced up, into the middle ear cavity, which is itself connected with various hollows or air cells in the bone surrounding it, such as the mastoid air cells. Among other vital structures of the middle ear is an exposed portion of the facial nerve. This nerve supplies the muscles of facial expression. Damage or infection to the middle ear can result in conditions such as deafness and facial paralysis.

The inner ear consists of the vestibule, the semicircular canals and the cochlea — which together form the bony labyrinth — and these are set into the bone of the base of the skull. This apparatus provides a sense of balance and awareness of position in space. The extremely fine vestibular membrane separates the inner ear from the middle ear. Infections of the middle ear, the surrounding bone and air cells, can involve the inner ear and this may result in otitis interna, causing imbalance, disorientation, distortion or even loss of hearing.

EPILOGUE

Water through the ages has been advocated as a means of maintaining health and treating disease. And so it is today. Water activity may be used either for therapy or for recreational swimming.

In the water, great feats are possible by the disabled, as for their normal peers, and we must ensure that the disabled are not denied access to this source of enjoyment by our ignorance or indifference.

Who would not be moved by the sight of the bright eyes and pride of a handicapped six-year-old boy who has achieved safe co-ordinated swimming before his normal elder brother? And who would begrudge the chairbound person the euphoria engendered by an hour of effortless rolling and somersaulting in the freedom of the water?

If a single statement could encompass the philosophy behind this monograph, it would be this: each and every individual who so wishes should have an opportunity to enjoy the freedom of movement that water ensures.

It is my hope that this monograph will provide you with the means to implement this philosophy.

REFERENCES

Arnhem D. and Sinclair W. (1979). *The Clumsy Child — a Program of Motor Therapy*, 2nd edn. St Louis, Miss.: C.V. Mosby.

Association of Swimming Therapy (1981). *Swimming for the Disabled.* Wakefield: E.P. Publishing.

Behrend H.J. (1960). Foreword. In *Hydrotherapy* (Finnerty F.G. and Corbitt T., eds.). London: Ungar.

Behrend H.J. (1963) Hydrotherapy. In *Medical Hydrology* (Licht S., ed.) pp.239–53. New Haven: Elizabeth Licht.

Bernstein N.R. (1976). *Emotional Care of the Facially Burned and Disfigured.* Boston: Little, Brown.

Best C. (1979). *Why Start with Infants?* Lecture given to Water Safety Symposium, Sydney, 3–4 October.

Bierman W. (1963). Physiologic changes produced by heat. In *Medical Hydrology* (Licht S., ed.) pp.78–116. New Haven: Elizabeth Licht.

Blanksby B.A. and Roberts D.M. (1981). *Guide for Teachers of Swimming.* Perth: University of Western Australia Press.

Boyle A.M. (1981). The Bad Ragaz ring method. *Physiotherapy*; **67**(9):265–8.

Brodal A. (1981). *Neurological Anatomy in Relation to Clinical Medicine*, 3rd edn. Oxford: Oxford University Press.

Bullock K. (1982). *Waterproofing Your Child.* Australia: Rigby.

Burden C. and Schurr P.H. (1976). *Understanding Epilepsy.* London: Crosby Lockwood Staples.

Campbell W.R. (1975). *Aqua Percept.* Pointe Claire: Wendy R. Campbell.

Campion M.J. (1983). Water activity based on the Halliwick method. In *Duffield's Exercise in Water* (Skinner A.T. and Thomson A.M., eds.), pp.180–96. London: Baillière Tindall.

Carmel P.W. (1974). Spina bifida. In *Spina Bifida in the Child with Disabling Illness* (Downey J. and Low N., eds.) pp.131–54. London: W.B. Saunders.

Carr J. and Shepherd R. (1980) *Physiotherapy in Disorders of the Brain.* London: Heinemann Medical.

Chaffee E.E. and Lytle I.M. (1980). *Basic Physiology and Anatomy*, 4th edn. Philadelphia: J.B. Lippincott.

Counsilman J.E. (1968). *The Science of Swimming.* New Jersey: Prentice Hall.

Cratty B.J. (1979). *Perceptual and Motor Development in Infants and Children*, 2nd edn. New Jersey: Prentice Hall.

Davis B. (1967). A technique of re-education in the treatment pool. *Physiotherapy;* **63**(2):57–9.

Downey J. (1971). Physiology of temperature regulation in man. In *Physiological Bases of Rehabilitation Medicine* (Downey J. and Darling R., eds.) pp.137–48. London: W.B. Saunders.

Elkington H. (1978. *Swimming — A Handbook for Teachers.* Cambridge: Cambridge University Press.

Erikson E.H. (1963). *Childhood and Society*, 2nd edn. New York: W.W. Norton.

Farmer T.W. (1975). *Paediatric Neurology*, 2nd edn. London: Harper & Row.

Finnerty F.G. and Corbitt T. (1960). *Hydrotherapy.* London: Ungar.

Fitch K.D. (1978). Swimming, medicine and asthma. In *Swimming Medicine*, Vol. IV (Eriksson B. and Furburg B., eds.) pp.16–31. Baltimore: University Park Press.

Fitch K.D. and Morton A.R. (1971). Specificity of exercise-induced asthma. *British Medical Journal;* **4**:577.

Foster M. (1982). *A Textbook of Physiology. Part III, The Central Nervous System*, 6th edn. London: Macmillan.

Freud S. (1955). *Beyond the Pleasure Principle*, standard edition, Vol. 18. London: Hogarth.

Gessell A., Ilg F.G. and Ames L. Bates (1974). *Infant and Child in the Culture Today* (revised edition). London: Hamish Hamilton.

Graham P.J. (1977). A child psychiatric approach. Behaviour disorders. In *Neurodevelopmental Problems in Early Childhood* (Drillien C.M. and Drummond M.B., eds.) Oxford: Blackwell Scientific.

Gray's Anatomy (1973). Hartwick R. and Williams P.L. (eds.). London: Longman.

Harris R. and McInnes M. (1963). Exercises in Water. In *Medical Hydrology* (Licht S., ed.) pp. 207–17. New Haven: Elizabeth Licht.

Heiniger M.C. and Randolph S.L. (1981). *Neurophysiological Concepts in Human Behaviour.* St Louis, Miss.: C.V. Mosby.

Held R. (1965). Plasticity in sensory-motor systems. *Scientific American;* **213**(5):84.

Holt K.S. (1965). *Assessment of Cerebral Palsy*. London: Lloyd Luke Medical.

Holt K.S. (1975). How and why children move. In *Movement and Child Development*, pp.1–7. London: Heinemann Medical/Spastic International Medical Publications.

Janig W. (1978). The autonomic nervous system, Section 8.5: The hypothalamus, osmolarity of the extracellular space, and the endocrine glands. In *Fundamentals of Neurophysiology*, 2nd edn (Schmidt R.F., ed.) pp.250–60. New York: Springer-Verlag.

Jennett W.B. and Teasdale G. (1981). *Management of Head Injuries*. Philadelphia: F.A. Davis.

Jolly H. (1975). *Book of Child Care*. London: George Allen & Unwin.

Kraus R. (1973). *Therapeutic Recreation Services — Principles and Practices*. Philadelphia: W.B. Saunders.

Lance J.W. and McLeod J.G. (1975). *A Physiological Approach to Clinical Neurology*, 2nd edn. Sydney: Butterworths.

Lindsay D. (1979). *The Importance of Swimming to Asthmatics*. Paper presented to Water Safety Symposium. Sydney: Department of Sport and Recreation.

MacDonald F.A. (1973). *Mechanics for Movement*. London: G. Bell & Sons.

McMillan J. (1975). Unpublished lecture material.

Matthews P.B.C. (1972). *Mammalian Muscle Receptors and their Central Actions*. London: Edward Arnold.

Matterson E. (1969). *This Little Puffin — Nursery Songs and Rhymes*. Harmondsworth: Puffin.

Mitchell L. (1977). *Simple Relaxation*. London: John Murray.

National Co-ordinating Committee on Swimming for the Disabled (1975). *Swimming and Epilepsy*. London: The Sports Council.

Oseid S., Kendall M., Larsen R.B. and Selbeck R. (1978). Physical activity programs for children with exercise-induced asthma. In *Swimming Medicine*, Vol. IV (Eriksson B. and Furburg B., eds.) pp.42–51. Baltimore: University Park Press.

Parry A. (1980). *Physiotherapy Assessment*. London: Croom Helm.

Phelan P. (1980). Asthma in children. *Medicine Australia*; Series 1, **23**:1639–47.

Piaget J. (1963). *Play, Dreams and Imitation in Childhood*. New York: Norton.

Price R.J. (1980). *Physical Education and the Physically Handicapped Child*. London: Lepus Books.

Reid M.J. (1975). *Handling the Disabled Child in Water — an Introduction*. Association of Paediatric Chartered Physiotherapists.

Reynell J.K. and Martin M.C. (1965). The response of children to physiotherapy. *Physiotherapy;* **51**(6): 186–9.

Rosenbloom L. (1975). The consequences of impaired movement — a hypothesis and review. In *Movement and Child Development* (Holt K., ed.) pp.8–13. London: Heinemann Medical.

Scrutton D. and Gilbertson M. (1975). *Physiotherapy in Paediatric Practice*. London: Butterworths.

Shapiro A.H. (1961). *Shape and Flow, the Fluid Dynamics of Drag*. London: Heinemann Educational.

Shepherd R. (1980). *Physiotherapy in Paediatrics*, 2nd edn. London: Heinemann Medical.

Sheridan M.D. (1977). *Spontaneous Play in Early Childhood from Birth to Six Years*. Slough: N.F.E.R.

Skinner A.T. and Thomson A.M. (eds.) (1983). *Duffield's Exercise in Water*, 3rd edn. London: Ballière Tindall.

Smith B.H. (1979). *Differential Diagnosis Neurology*. New York: Acro.

Smith D.W. and Bierman E.L. (1973). *The Biologic Ages of Man — From Conception Through Old Age*. Philadelphia: W.B. Saunders.

Stallibrass A. (1977). *The Self-respecting Child — A Study of Children's Play and Development*. Ringwood: Penguin (Australia).

Stone F.H. (1976). *Psychiatry and the Paediatrician*. London: Butterworths.

Sullivan P.E., Markos P.D. and Minor M.A.D. (1982). *An Integrated Approach to Therapeutic Exercise — Theory and Clinical Application*. Reston: Reston Publishing.

Trussell E.C. (1971). *Guidelines for Teaching the Disabled to Swim*. Dudley: Netherton Printers for Swimming Teacher's Association.

Wilson I.H. and Kasch F.W. (1963). Medical aspects of swimming. In *Medical Hydrology* (Licht S., ed.) pp.229–38. New Haven: Elizabeth Licht.

FURTHER READING

Davies P.A., Drillien C.M., Foley J., Bryant K.M., Nash M.I. and Mulhall Egan J. (1977). Cerebral palsy. In *Neurodevelopmental Problems in Early Childhood* (Drillien C.M. and Drummond M.B., eds.) pp.259–334. Oxford: Blackwell Scientific.

Holt K.S. (1977). *Developmental Paediatrics*. London: Butterworths.

Jennett W.B. (1981). Epidemiology of head injuries. In *Head Injuries — An Integrated Approach* (Dinning T.A.R. and Connelly T.J., eds.) pp.2–8. Brisbane: John Wiley.

McGraw-Hill Encyclopaedia of Science and Technology (1971). New York: McGraw-Hill.

Massey B.S. (1979). *Mechanics of Fluid*, 4th edn. London: Van Nostrand Reinhold.

Van Nostrand's Scientific Encyclopaedia, 4th edn (1968). London: Van Nostrand.

INDEX